To Kris Hansen
From Philip Lesly

May 13, 1975

The people factor
Managing the human climate

The people factor
Managing the
human climate

PHILIP LESLY

 1974

DOW JONES-IRWIN, INC.
Homewood, Illinois 60430

First Printing, January 1974

ISBN 0-87094-069-4
Library of Congress Catalog Card No. 73–89119
Printed in the United States of America

To Craig, Carole,
Elizabeth, and Melissa

Introduction

Over the past several years it has become apparent that many officials of our institutions and corporations are finding a widening chasm between themselves and the publics they deal with.

In an era when most men and women seem to have become assertive, when every kind of viewpoint has a movement and a loud voice, when every pillar in our social structure is under attack, this gap is threatening to undermine all of our organizations and the society they compose. It seems not only pertinent but urgent that the causes of this estrangement be diagnosed, and a course of treatment sought.

This book has evolved from my writing and my experience in helping a number of large organizations cope with the human climate in which they must function, plus a growing awareness of the way professional managers are speeding toward mastery of all the factors of operating an organization—except the one that may doom it.

Management might seem to an uncritical observer to have become our new priesthood. There are thousands of books and manuals devoted to it. There are lavishly financed graduate schools, luxuriously outfitted centers for advanced training, a library of periodicals, sophisticated series of cassettes, junkets for further study in most corners of the world, booklets, teaching materials, and other tools. Young people and people not so young pay obeisance at the shrines of management lore.

There is a profession of management for business. Professional management in government has been endorsed by presidents of the United States. There are professional managers for medical services, hospitals, and schools. Unions are training their future leaders in the techniques of management. And efficient management in the home is heralded as the means by which women can cope with boredom and be freed to fulfill themselves.

The concept behind almost all of these is that management is a discipline that requires all factors in an organization's operations to be rendered as knowable and measurable as possible, that management deals with information—which becomes the data of the data processing that the process of management increasingly pivots on. Data for the computers, the financial statements, the proposals and reports are, by definition and by the nature of computers, numbers—the most tangible and measurable of facts. Since the computer on which much of management depends requires numerical data, it is a short step to the concept that "if it can't be counted it doesn't count."

In higher education for management, the gospel is the case-study method, which approaches each topic as an interplay of the tangible facts involved. Where the vagaries and immeasurabilities of human attitudes intrude, they tend to be treated as mutations—nuisance factors that must be neutralized so the tangible factors can proceed undisturbed to a measurable result.

Where the human factor is recognized, it tends to be shaped into the same mold as the tangibles, with charts. Even the classic work by Douglas McGregor in defining the X and Y approaches to management of personnel—a milestone in dealing with the nuances of human responses—has been widely interpreted through the use of charts and diagrams.

In other cases where the human factor is seen to be important, it is covered under "communications," along with such tools of management as transportation, purchasing, or finance.

Some, but comparatively few, discerning managers recognize that the total scope of attitudes of their publics is the encompassing atmosphere in which all other factors function, and determines how they will succeed—that it is, in fact, *the human climate* that determines how all elements will grow or wither. That human climate is as vital and as all-encompassing a consideration for management as the weather climate is for the farmer.

It has become increasingly evident to me that there is a growing gap between many managers and the groups whose attitudes make up their human climate.

Most managers tend to look at the functions intended to deal with the human climate as tools, rather than as an over-all determinant.

There are many managers who have recognized the importance of the people factor and have adjusted their outlook accordingly. They keep the human-climate factors in mind at all times. They include expert counsel and input on the human climate in the considerations on which they base their decisions. They have demonstrated by the wisdom of this awareness that there is hope for its being achieved by other managers.

Since the attitudes of the publics are increasingly becoming the decisive factors in the future of all our institutions, I hope that spelling out what is involved and giving some guidelines for coping with them will contribute to the future of our society.

The analysis and direction aimed at by this book seem to be overdue. I hope it will stimulate further consideration and development among thoughtful people interested in helping make our society work and those who have the awesome responsibility for managing the fundamental structures that make it up.

December 1973   Philip Lesly

Acknowledgments

Appreciation is due the *Journal of Marketing,* and *PR Reporter* for permission to quote material from articles that have appeared therein; and to Prentice-Hall, Inc. for permission to cite segments of *Lesly's Public Relations Handbook.*

Thoughtful comment and encouragement have come from many people, among them Harry Heltzer, Glen Perry, Richard R. Connaroe, Robert N. Thurston, Virginia Barnes, Douglas Mueller, Charles H. Prout, Charles F. Barber, Robert L. Barbour, Jack O'Dwyer, Emil Hubka, John E. Fletcher, Chester Burger, Ralph A. Rieves, D. Christopher Whittle, Harold Brayman, Morton J. Simon, Walter W. Reed, Guenther Baumgart, Roy Leffingwell, Terry Mayer, Dr. Rex F. Harlow, Dr. Carl F. Hawver, Harold Burson, W. Howard Chase, Donald Pitti, Henry G. Harper, John N. DeBoice, John E. Fields, Nicholas Biro, Denny Griswold, Jim Atkins, Howard P. Hudson, Dr. Albert Walker, and Anne R. Warner.

Contributions of patience, alertness, and help with the manuscript have come from staff members Susanne Scharding, Veronica Woerner, and Janis Young.

Contents

SECTION I The stormy new human climate

chapter 1 The presumption of guilt

THERE have been various "takeoff points" in the history of man's struggle from the roving hunter to the present complex Western way of life. The basis for one of these undoubtedly was the American genius for development of many forms of organization. A cooperating group of people with like objectives was found to have infinitely more capability for achievement than the sum of those individuals separately.

In effect, the advanced American civilization that, until recently, has been the envy of almost all the world evolved into a society not only of individuals but of organizations that interrelate with each other.

One part of the "American miracle" was the way this society of organizations, each with its disciplines, at the same time produced the greatest degree of individual freedom and the greatest range of individual choice of any major society in history.

The concept of the corporate entity arose in Europe, but it found its greatest fulfillment in the United States in the latter part of the 19th century and in the 20th century. American law developed a structure that encouraged joint organizations —corporations, associations, and others—to undertake and accomplish what their individual members could not hope to do.

Americans came from the start to their instinct for organizing together. The Mayflower Compact was signed even before the landing. As early as 1835, Alexis de Tocqueville remarked on the unique propensity of Americans in all walks of life to become joiners and cooperators.

Corporations were the first and most prominent enterprises, their history going back to the groups that were established to encourage settlement of this savage and undeveloped land. But it was not long before there were formed colleges that grew in organizational complexity into universities; professional and trade associations; religious groups that tied together the interests of individual churches; and unions of workers that blossomed into formidable national organizations.

Even in his social life the American turned to the organization. The Masons, Shriners, Elks, Moose, Odd Fellows, Rotarians, Kiwanians, Lions, and many others were formed to fill an appetite and a need between the time of the simple village, where everyone knew everyone else, to the time of our present vast megalopolitan communities and mass communications.

American society, and especially business leaders, thus created a "systems society" in which individuals belonged to various organizations devoted to their various interests—economic, spiritual, social, political—and the organizations worked and competed together. The result was a sort of benign tension in which the individual gave up some of his autonomy to gain the benefits that only the organizations could provide, and the organizations went through a give-and-take in achieving their goals.

The result often found some unfortunate consequences, and some losers along with the many winners. It produced periods of the "malefactors of great wealth," the "economic royalists," the Ku Klux Klan, and other aberrations. It has been marked by serious abuses of ethics and human rights in all eras, including the present one. But it also produced the most dynamic society in history, in which the overwhelming majority of individuals not only participated but visibly improved their economic and social lot more rapidly than anywhere else.

Clearly, it was a part of the American achievement that almost all its people saw the value of organizations and of unity among members of organizations for the orderly achievement of mutual goals.

A historic shift

But now the organizations and the synergistic economic power they have made possible are not only often frustrated in their efforts to carry on their functions; they are under widespread attack.

The great American tradition that an institution, like an individual, was innocent until proved guilty has been superseded by a public climate that permits and even encourages attacks on all institutions, with the presumption of their guilt until they have gone through an inquisition.

Militant groups have shut down universities and meetings of organizations with impunity. Welfare mothers have tied up courts. Government agencies have damaged businesses by aggressive action that months or years later has proved to be unwarranted. Some of the media are dedicated to finding charges they can throw at various institutions before any hearing on the issues and without recourse when the charges prove to be erroneous.

The presumption of guilt has now become a major motivation within the activist segment of society and a portion of the legal profession. They now openly advocate the filing of hundreds of thousands of lawsuits, putting organizations on the defensive regardless of the merits of the cases.

As a result, managers in many corporations and organizations now base their judgments as much on whether new hostilities will be hurled at them as on the merits of the matter at hand. A major portion of the time of management must be devoted to forestalling and coping with attacks on them. And a major part of the cost of goods and services is devoted to the unproductive legal, clerical, and other activities required to deal with this new aberration in the human climate.

Not only are private organizations under attack; there is a strong trend toward loading the blame on them for the consequences of actions they undertook reluctantly or not at all.

• Inflation is largely due to spending by government and industry in pursuing early solutions to massive problems, such as instant elimination of inequality, immediate provision of good living for all, and assured health for the poor and the aged; as well as to spending in Southeast Asia. But those who proposed and pushed through these ventures are blaming the private sector for high prices.

• Power shortages result from many factors, including policies dealing with supply and pricing that are aimed at keeping costs low to the consumer, stringent restrictions on new exploration and transportation, and unrestricted encouragement of cars and conveniences for everyone, as well as practices of the petroleum and utility industries. But while oil remains unshipped from Alaska, offshore drilling is cut back, refineries can't be built, and power stations take years for approval, the cry is being heard that the fault for power shortages lies with business.

Management—always present-minded and inherently optimistic—thus often is trapped into being spotlighted as the source of unattainable hopes . . . and then castigated when the expectations aren't fulfilled.

They're damned if they do and damned if they don't; but they're damned, damned, damned in a human climate that now often seeks its scapegoats among the most visible and most powerful, rather than that traditional source of scapegoats, the isolated and oppressed.

chapter 2 The penalty for responsibility

THOSE who have nothing to lose can be irresponsible with impunity.

When the Federal Trade Commission accuses duPont of falsifying advertising for its Xerex antifreeze and then, many months later, withdraws its charge as unfounded, the members of the FTC and its staff go blithely on to their next case. The company pays the penalty for being attacked.

When students take over the administration building of a university, their first demand is for immunity from prosecution. When the hassle is over they go on without penalty, while the university struggles to make up its losses in money and educational purpose.

When a band of Indians devastates the Bureau of Indian Affairs, the taxpayers are confronted with costs of millions of dollars, but the perpetrators are left unscathed.

When a group of irresponsible activists ties up a court for months and disrupts its operations, the judge is castigated and the disrupters go free.

Those who are trained to withhold judgment until the facts are in . . . to give precedence to reason over passion . . . to base

7

their case on merits rather than on emotion are the most vulnerable to activist dissent.

The high level of responsibility that marks most established people—college presidents, physicians, clergymen, corporate executives, most government officials—leads them to abhor public combat. A climate that not only condones but rewards combativeness puts the responsible members of society at a disadvantage.

In an age of activism and visibility, a field or organization with high standards, which deplores aggression and works in dignified silence, is a sitting duck. Lawyers, doctors, academicians, and business statesmen who scorn efforts to capture favorable attention face being swept into subjugation by the nature of the times.

Managers of our institutions become leaders and have the capability of operating large and complex institutions for the very reason that they exhibit unusual self-control and restraint.

They are able to put long-term values before their immediate gratifications.

They give thought to how their present actions will affect people's regard for what they do and say in the future.

These traits are admirable in what has been the normal pattern of our social dynamics, but they make the manager vulnerable to attacks from those who can hit and run with nothing to lose. The flaws of modern business are especially susceptible to attack, and they have been ready targets of many groups and individuals.

Traits that led to success in a simpler society can predispose to disaster in our present society unless modified with sensitivity to today's human climate.

This is a consequence of the extremism of "democracy" —never foreseen by the most visionary of the founders of our democratic society—that seeks to give a voice and power to everyone on every issue and in the running of every institution, regardless of his merit in serving society or ability.

Retaining a sense of responsibility and a concern for future reputation while staving off the virulence of attacks is a new requirement that faces the modern manager. It is as severe and crucial a challenge as any that has ever been faced by leaders of our institutions.

chapter 3   The dangers of executive isolation

Forces that are increasing the isolation of management people from what is really happening may be among the greatest threats to survival of our economic and social system.

In past times, the élite who lived in isolated and entrenched comfort lost touch with the real currents of change and were swept aside. There is such a danger today. The more successful management has been in creating new benefits for the populace, the more it has become out of touch with what all those people out there are really thinking.

Executives who need outside viewpoints pressed on them even more are, instead, increasingly moving into stainless steel towers and building increasingly ingrown organizations.

Managers are uncomfortably aware that there are strong currents in the human climate that are alien to them. They know that many of the young people see business as mechanistic, computerized, hard-headed, "tough minded"—suspicious of new ideas and uncomfortable with intangibles such as the attitudes and aspirations of people.

They have been made aware of the bewildering alienation of

minority groups, which are putting stresses on the whole fabric of our society because they want more and are not clear about whom they want it from or how.

They are uneasy with the growing gap in value judgments.

Economic and material advancement per se, which has been the main thrust of their lives since childhood, is now openly rejected by millions.

They are faced with pressures to reduce deaths on the highways, prevent the poisoning of the air and water, forestall congestion created by so much "progress" that livability is threatened. They are confronted by the longing for beauty and hedonism that calls for more leisure time rather than more dedication to work.

This estrangement between the executives who make our modern world function and all of those people out there is especially ironic. For it is the organizations that are threatened with becoming the victims of their own success. As they achieve new benefits, comforts, and resources for humanity, they also create new aspirations and expectations among the people.

What an earlier generation considered utopian dreams have been made by the progress of business into current demands —and business is castigated if it does not readily provide them.

Similarly, the medical and pharmaceutical fields are being pilloried because they have made such prodigious strides that the public views the miracles of good health care not as privileges but as rights to which everyone is entitled, at little or no cost.

The colleges have done so well in establishing the value of higher education that they are being forced to revolutionize themselves to provide a college education for almost everyone, again at little or no cost.

Causes of isolation

This estrangement is a direct consequence of the growth and complexity of our institutions.

1. Physical isolation

As organizations grow and prosper, the key executives tend to live in steel-and-glass towers with private banks of elevators leading to the top floor so they won't be crowded in with the help.

They eat in superexecutive dining rooms so they won't have to see department heads at lunch.

They have company airplanes so they won't have to fly on a commercial airline and sit next to someone who earns only $40,-000 a year.

They go to vacation resorts and hunting lodges to which only businessmen in the rarefied tax brackets are invited.

They belong to the most exclusive clubs in each city and have chauffered cars so they won't have to listen to cab drivers.

When they ask to see a $30,000-a-year executive, he feels as though he is visiting the throne room. Such a meeting hardly represents a free exchange of personalities and ideas.

2. Educational conformity

Although the era when business leaders came out of only one social class is largely over, they now tend more and more to come out of the same training pattern. They go to a good college and take an M.B.A. or Advanced Management Course at Harvard, Stanford, Wharton, or the like. Then, to "keep up with the times," they take a short course in computers or the Critical Path Method. They get out of touch with what ordinary people are thinking and doing.

3. Corporate centralization

There is a trend toward centralizing the total corporate power structure.

Although the concerns of our corporations are rapidly decentralizing to diverse areas of the country and to most corners of the world, executive orientation is becoming increasingly centralized. Problems arise in Washington, Birmingham, Los Angeles, London, Cairo, Tokyo, Rio. Yet more and more executives act as though the focal point of the world is in the tight circle within 40 miles of New York.

Even the growing number of organizations who are fleeing Manhattan tend to establish their redoubts on its outskirts.

Centralization of finance and communications—two vital keys to executive functioning—is constantly increasing in the New York area. Yet it is the least typical city in the United States in thought as well as in all other ways.

4. Regional chauvinism

Another kind of geographic isolation is the other side of this coin. That is regionalism, even in a company that operates nationally and internationally. In an age when what an Arab thinks of a company can have grave consequences, a majority of managers still give in to the temptation to think and act like their friends and neighbors. The geographic chauvinism between Californians, Texans, New Englanders, and others is still marked.

5. Hiring habits

Despite the move toward open hiring and the deliberate acceleration of progress for some women and minority members, there is still isolation caused by hiring habits.

Almost everyone has the natural tendency to hire people who impress him as meeting his standards and his way of approaching things. What this really means is hiring people in one's own image.

And then there is the tendency to promote those people who best catch on to what the manager approves. Thus, future managers tend to be preselected because they are like their predecessors, and are rewarded and promoted to the degree that they perform like their predecessors. This builds in isolation from the rapidly changing character of our population, making it more difficult to absorb and advance the neglected minorities. And it builds in a time lag: the new generation of management is much like the old one, but a generation late, even before it gets to be management.

Today, one generation is a long time when change is so rapid and so sweeping. Few individuals, firms, or organizations can ride out even one generation, holding to a pattern that was set in the past.

Everyone is trained in one generation and must function professionally a generation later. What used to take a generation to change or occur now often changes in two or three years.

6. Ingrown operations

There is a penchant for making corporate structures homogeneous.

The bigger an organization becomes, the more it tends to feel it should be self-contained and self-sufficient. Many large organizations try to have everything possible done by their own employees. The trend to the fee system in advertising, for instance, instead of compensation of advertising agencies through commissions paid by the media, may be a stepping-stone to deciding which agency functions can be absorbed by the company instead of being done by "outsiders."

Helping to make certain that divisional managers will not get any outside viewpoint is the way a number of large firms have established captive "consultants" in various fields. They are usually expected to "compete" for the assignments of the company's units, but it is competition comparable to a Russian election.

When the need as now is to get *diverse* thinking and the broadest possible experience in all fields, this trend to internalization is comparable to the extreme nationalism of France or the states' rights approach to water resources.

The Watergate affair was a dramatic demonstration of how serious this ingrown isolation can be. An organization that is tight and ingrown is vulnerable to misinformation, misreading of the human climate that it must exist in, misconstruing of events, and distortion to protect personal interests. Mitchell, Haldeman, and Ehrlichman comprised an exceptionally close ring of advisers to the President and were especially effective in making certain that few outside voices or viewpoints reached him. The consequences should be an object lesson to managers for all time.

7. Focus on immediacy

A less obvious but equally virulent form of executive isolation is the strong polarization toward *now*—the results for *this* quarter and *this* year.

Many managers talk freely about living in the fastest changing period in history—but then make decisions on the basis of how good immediate profit and loss statements will look.

8. Standardization

There is a trend toward *standardization* that results in cutting managements off from changing conditions.

Because products, production methods, purchasing controls, and the like can be handled by data processing and automation, they tend to become more and more alike.

Companies even send their people to the same meetings of the American Management Association to be sure they know the same methods and techniques and are less likely to go off doing original or untried things.

Rigidity of thinking around methods and tools that can be cataloged, computerized, and predicted is a major form of isolation.

9. Lack of communication

Isolated executives trained to be "tough minded" tend to become less and less able to communicate with those unlike them. They try to communicate *at* people—to issue directives, make statements of what people should think—without realizing that communication is a *transaction*. It involves a continuous-loop process of transmission, feedback, and adjustment.

No manager can communicate a laissez-faire social philosophy into the mind of a worker who grew up with no prospect of going either to college or to a winter home in Palm Beach.

The extent of this failure to communicate is visible in the estrangement of business from many of the brightest members of the younger generation.

The absence on boards of directors of outside thinkers whose function is to inject bridges of understanding with outside groups is one of the most common reasons that many organizations find the new human climate stormy.

chapter 4 Needed: A Darwin for enterprise

In many corporate executive offices, two topics now accompany profitability as major concerns:

1. "Corporate responsibility," covering the gamut of the responses of business to the social issues of our time;
2. The failure of business to communicate the need for profits, the importance of free enterprise, and the role of business in achieving our society's goals.

Corporate responsibility is seen as the active role of the company in coping with the problems of society: pollution, product quality and safety, illness, discrimination against women and minorities, crime and violence, poverty, alcoholism and drugs, to name some of them. In all these areas, obviously much more needs to be done.

During the intensive search of the corporate soul, corporations are in two senses becoming more socialized. They are moving to become real forces in reshaping our social structure; and their independence from government is being reduced.

From the podium, in press meetings, and in board rooms, the complaint is heard that American business is not getting across

.its role as "free enterprise" . . . that the blessings that spring from free enterprise are not appreciated by the benefited millions.

• John D. Harper, chairman, Aluminum Corporation of America, expressed this feeling: "Business seems to have lost its voice just when it needs it most."[1]

• Elisha Gray II, Chairman of the Finance Committee of Whirlpool Corporation, has been a leader in advocating greater attention by business to the complaints of consumers and the disquiet among the public about the role of business. He said: "The American electorate will largely dismantle the free-enterprise system in the next ten years if we businessmen continue to stand mute."[2]

A talk by Richard C. Gerstenberg, chairman of General Motors, before the 1971 Congress of American Industry conducted by the National Association of Manufacturers was titled: "The Importance of Profits and Free Enterprise."

Mr. Gerstenberg combined a cogent explanation of the need for profits with a call for better communication of business' role. "You and I know," he said, "that profits are to free enterprise what oats are to the racehorse—essential both as a reward and as a fuel for continued competition."

Such a relation of "profits"—the tangible and fundamental incentive of business—with "free enterprise," an abstract concept that has never been clear to the public and is least clear now, is a common theme in business.

But if "free enterprise" ever was an apt description, it becomes less apt every day. Increasingly, our efforts are going into areas where "enterprise" is an alien term, but "incentive" is vital: hospitals and medical care, schools, social services, public services such as police and sanitation, and other fields where profit *in*

---

[1] Footnotes are located at the end of the book.

dollars is a secondary concern, at best.[3] All of these have their vital incentives, not primarily financial but still forceful in getting their tasks done.

Defining the nature of enterprise

It seems time to question whether the movement of business to meet society's problems and the term "free enterprise" are compatible. If business lacks credibility among academicians and youth, a major reason may be this inconsistency between how it really functions and its use of "free enterprise" as a description.

Business has been clamoring for a Demosthenes, who could utter "the word" and sway everyone to its viewpoint. It needs instead its Darwin, who can size up all the existing factors and, in the face of charges of heresy, show business what it really is: how it has evolved, its present nature, where it is going. Business may have its illusions of divine conception shattered; but it will gain a cosmology that it can live with and, even more important, that can be made credible to all of its publics.

It is clear that efforts to communicate the functions and value of business have failed. Every known poll shows that confidence in business' role as a moving factor in our society has been dropping drastically.[4]

What are the reasons?

In summary, in some areas business has not performed adequately in the public interest. This is being improved rapidly, yet the level of public regard continues to fall. Clearly, business has failed in its communications because most of the basic requirements of a sound mass-communication effort have been violated or ignored. So the public does not give it credit even for what it has done—and is unlikely to laud further efforts toward responsibility when they come.

This failure to gain public awareness of their problems and

improvements occurs with all institutions—education, government, labor, health care, the legal system, the church—but it is most glaring in business. It is businessmen, after all, who most often propound the need to "get across" their story and have the means most readily available.

Destructive and constructive factors

Understanding the challenges facing business in dealing with the pressures for responsibility and the failures of communication calls for a review of destructive and constructive factors and their effects:

1. Errors that blight the public attitude toward business:
    a. Errors of commission.
    b. Errors of omission.
    c. Errors of communication in regard to problems
2. Constructive actions and communications.

Errors of commission

These include a wide range of practices that have been built by business' critics into a bill of particulars to indict business. Some examples are:

- Charges against such firms as U.S. Plywood-Champion Papers, Jones & Laughlin Steel, Republic Steel, Armco Steel, Kennebec River Pulp & Paper, Bettinger Corporation, J. J. O'Donnell Woolens, and Union Pacific Railroad for extensive and continuous pollution of waterways.

- Revelation that for about 80 years, prior to the election of the present chairman, Charles F. Barber, American Smelting & Refining Company had done nothing about a massive build-up of lead in the ground and air near its El Paso smelter.

- Massive cost overruns by defense contractors who had "bought in" on contracts by apparently deliberately underquoting bids, climaxing with the bailout of Lockheed.
- Alleged misrepresentation or suppression of research data that reflected unfavorably on drugs, such as MER/29 by William S. Merrell Company.
- Cynical efforts to cash in on issues of responsibility, such as the promotion of Ecolo-G as a safe nonphosphate detergent and the promotion of some artificial cream products with high fat content as "healthful" substitutes for real cream.

Errors of omission

One senses an obsession with self-criticism in the frequency with which business leaders regret the failure to anticipate the wave of accusations or to nail criticisms before they caught on.

- There was almost no challenge to constant assertions by critics that, if we could land a man on the moon, by applying the same dedication and concentration of effort we could solve all our social problems on earth . . . and by implication, that it was the establishment's bullheaded insensitivity to the problems that stood in the way.
- Especially rued is the failure to communicate about business as a vital part of our society. This was expressed by William V. Luneberg, president of American Motors: "As businessmen, we have been telling ourselves for a long time that we ought to improve our communications skills. But we haven't done so, probably because we have continued to feel that time could be better spent on problems of research, production, and marketing. We have paid a price for this attitude, and the price is going to keep going up. We had better at last make up our minds to do a better job."[5]

Errors of communication

The zeal for communication as a cure for problems often takes on the aura of expectations from "miracle drugs."

One aspect might be called the "communicate-problems-away" approach.

- Amtrak started a major effort to use words to sell its passenger railroad service before any substantial move was made to upgrade the service. Its failure was followed by requests for larger government subsidies.

- The mining industry is one of the most besieged of all, being accused of marring the face of the countryside, building up unsightly and dangerous hills of sludge, befouling water with waste, and continuing some unsafe practices. Rather than address alleviation of these problems, the prescription given before a meeting of the American Mining Congress by its president, Gilbert E. Dwyer, president of Kennecott Copper, was: ". . . this industry has a bigger role to play in society than the role of whipping boy for special interests. And to be able to play our proper role, we must first make it understood."

- The plastics industry has been embroiled in a number of charges involving packaging, disposal, and contamination. Yet the Plastics Council was formed with this declared purpose: ". . . to inform and remind opinion leaders of the inherent values of plastics to our society and to correct some of the misconceptions currently prevalent, particularly in regard to plastics and the environment."

- The Tobacco Institute continues to devote major efforts to reasserting doubts about worldwide medical findings implicating cigarettes as a cause factor in various illnesses.

- Potlach Forests ran the now famous advertisement, "It Cost Us a Bundle but the Clearwater River Still Runs Clear." Skeptical students investigated, and *Newsweek* showed that the photo in the ad was taken 50 miles upstream. The area near the paper mill was described as looking like a cesspool.[6]

• Standard Oil (California) spent $13,000,000 in 1970 alone advertising its F-310 gasoline as "the most outstanding development in automotive fuel in years." Photos showed a black balloon filled with exhaust from other gasoline and an almost clear balloon with exhaust from F-310. A furor of accusations about the authenticity of the tests, the photos, and the claims was at this writing still stirring.[7]

• The most common mistake in trying to communicate problems away involves the use of institutional advertising, as we shall see in Chapter 42. Most such advertising tends to be an effort to "put across" ideas that the advertiser wants very much to have his audience accept. His self-interest is evident and so is the fact that he has spent a lot of money to try to impose his thinking on the audience. With willingness to accept the credibility of organizations at a low level, such one-directional arguments tend not only to be rejected, but to create resentment. This is not communication but exhortation, even in its most cosmetic and subtle forms.

Another type of communications mistake can be called the "do versus say" approach.

• Edward J. Gerrity, senior vice president of ITT, said before the Financial Communications Society of New York a few months before his company became the center of multiple controversies about its practices and communications at home and abroad: "There are two prerequisites [for a corporate relations man who is a real part of the top-management process]: first, a chief executive who knows and respects the power of public opinion; second, a corporate relations staff (with) sound judgment, know-how, creative imagination, and a concept of the role of corporate relations. . . ."8

• Many of the same business leaders who give public testimony to the need for recognizing that our economy is really a profit *and loss* system also supported the bail-outs of Lockheed and the Pennsylvania Railroad from the consequences of their losses.

• Those who advocate substantial programs of drug-abuse education continue to oppose restricting advertising that depicts pill-popping as an easy and acceptable way to cope with many of life's problems.

Attempts to deal with problems by trying to cover up or to distort cause the spread of cynicism, when they are revealed.

• Professor Yale Brozen of the University of Chicago received widespread attention for a speech he delivered defending many advertising practices and excoriating the tactics of the Federal Trade Commission. Then it was revealed that he was retained as a consultant by the public relations firm for ITT Continental Baking—a primary target of the FTC's efforts. Certainly the effect would have been more securely made if his interest in the arguments given had been clear.

• The entire saga of the ITT case involving the campaign contribution to the Republican Party and the decisions involving antitrust cases pending against the company conditioned the public to believe the most damaging accusations made by critics about the tactics of big business.

• Revelations of funds contributed surreptitiously or illegally to the campaign to re-elect President Nixon in 1972 were followed by charges of favoritism by his administration toward some of the donors. Such devious maneuvers spotlighted public suspicions about the irresponsibilities of the private sector.

• A lone activist who took the name "The Fox" became a Robin
Hood of environmentalism by making dramatic sneak attacks
on various companies in the Chicago area that were accused of
polluting the air and water. Because he was trying to expose
efforts to cover up such practices, he became a folk hero far
beyond Chicago.

We shall examine later some constructive actions and communications techniques that can gain for America's organizations
the kind of public understanding of their nature that Darwin
achieved for the nature of living organisms.

chapter 5 The mass production of expectations

Many of the problems of our human climate are related to one fact: *Our whole society has grossly overbuilt its expectations of what can be achieved and provided.*

We lose sight of our many great advances, any one of which would have been monumental in past societies.

Life expectancy has gone up more than 50 percent in the last two generations, and most of the dreaded maladies that all previous mankind felt were unavoidable have been conquered or alleviated.

The proportion of families at the poverty level has been reduced by more than 40 percent in only eight years.

The scope of what the individual can span in his life has been broadened immeasurably.

Wonders that would have been miracles to our grandparents now come so frequently that we scarcely pay attention to them while we clamor for new miracles not yet in our grasp.

John Kenneth Galbraith, although himself one of the greatest inflators of unattainable expectations, said in *The Liberal Hour:* "If we foster great expectations, we must count on deep disillusion."

Though our society is held in awe throughout the world for its mass production of goods, our mass production of expectations may be the trait that will distinguish us in history.

The universal grasp for the public's favor has become a spiral of allures and promises in all our media, in the cascade of advertising messages that engulfs us, in many of the public relations efforts of our industries and governments, in political platforms and promulgations, in the claims for omnipotence of our schools and colleges.

Charles Reich in *The Greening of America* points out that advertising is capable "of creating a maximum of dissatisfaction and a minimum willingness to accept the drudgery of life."

The role of manipulative government is depicted by Peter Drucker in *The Age of Discontinuity:*

. . . the welfare state promised a great deal more than to provide social services. It promised to create a new and happy society, to release creative energies, and to do away with ugliness and envy and strife. . . .

During the past three decades, Federal payments to the big cities have increased almost a hundredfold for all kinds of programs. But results from the incredible dollar flood into the cities are singularly unimpressive. What's impressive is the administrative incompetence. We now have 10 times as many government agencies concerned with city problems as we had in 1939. We've increased by a factor of a thousand or so the number of reports and papers that have to be filled out before anything can be done. Social workers in New York City spend about 70 or 80 percent of their time filling out papers—for Washington, for the state government in Albany, and for New York City. No more than 20 or 30 percent of their time, about an hour and a half a day, is available for their clients, the poor.

The vague promises of the welfare state, said Professor Arthur Case, are "the utopium of the people."

The accumulation of illusion

The presentation of the ideal and the ease of attaining it permeate every niche of our lives. Our success in depicting the girl with impudent breasts and imprudent buttocks as the norm has destroyed the ability of millions of men to find plentiful joys in girls with an inch less here and an inch more there. The cult of youth that is one of our best-sold concepts assures that everyone will feel neurotic strains with time. In every aspect of our lives, reality is so much less glamorous than the gilded illusions, scarcely anyone settles for it in his human relations. Even the pulpits, having more difficulty selling a dull and sexless heaven, are turning to sanctifying a kingdom of copious copulation on earth.

Henry Steele Commager said in *America in Perspective:*

. . . America was the land of perfectionism. The American knew that nothing was impossible, in this brave new world, and history confirmed his intuition. Progress was not, to him, a mere philosophical ideal but a commonplace of experience, and he could not understand why foreigners should see vulgar realities where he saw visions. He was outraged at any failure, at any imperfection even, could not tolerate a depression or a military defeat, could not acquiesce in any inadequacy of culture.

In other societies such an outpouring of delusions would not be possible. It is only where miracles are constantly occurring, where so much happens for improvement, that the people can be so susceptible to being conned.

It is advancement and the *visibility* of advancement that stirs desires. Like Shakespeare's Cleopatra, our satisfactions whet the very appetites they slake.

Americans are known everywhere for their speed in accepting the new and their readiness to change. They used to expect miracles tomorrow. Now they protest when they are not delivered today.

The feeling that we are entitled to whatever has been held

before us has led us impatiently to take matters into our own hands and accounts for the self-fulfillment of expectations through shoplifting, embezzlement, street crime, and burglary; the outpourings of rage in vandalism, assault, and militance.

"The hoped-for changes from poverty to affluence, from subjection to freedom, from work to leisure do not enhance social stability but threaten social dissolution," said Eric Hoffer in *The Temper of Our Time.*

"The exaggerated promises have upset the normal human willingness to accept the fact that there are no sudden, that there are no universal, remedies for the hardness of the human condition on this planet," said Walter Lippmann.

Not only are we beguiled into expecting that we are entitled to immunity from harm (three quarters of us refuse to use the seat belts that are readily at hand in our cars) and from illness (most disease is self-imposed by our drinking, smoking, miseating, dissipating, laziness, and sleeplessness). We are so assured of the presence of health miracles that we consume billions of pills and potions, and sue our doctors when we don't get well instantly from whatever ails us.

And now the maladies of the spirit are expected to disappear, too, the pleasant and easy way, in touching and fondling and encountering others who join us in a revel of mutual neuroticism. Encounter therapy is called the "human potential movement," as if rubbing against each other is what human aspirations are all about.

If the magic of pills or physicians or public self-immolation and fondling don't work, we turn to the magic of magic. We are in the midst of an orgy of the occult, a deliberate reach for illusions to replace the deflated delusions all around us. Since the complicated world of reality goes stubbornly on becoming more complex, millions are turning avidly to simple and "visible" answers. Since man on earth clearly is not master of his fate, then the stars must be . . . or the devil . . . or tarot cards . . . or gurus in far-off India who are not bogged down in our mechanized society . . . or maybe "love."

This verges on the ultimate cop-out, the extreme of antireality and reaction against involvement. To expect the powers of the future to be controlled by the stars or ouija boards or tarot cards or incantations in the night is to expect nothing from the established systems. In fact, if there were an establishment in control of our society, it could do no better for itself than to encourage the flight to the occult as a diversion from activism.

We are the middlemen in the paradox that besets those who woo us. "Those who would transform a nation or the world . . . must know how to kindle and fan an extravagant hope," Eric Hoffer tells us in *The True Believer*.

But the wisdom of Montaigne, that "there is no greater enemy of those who would please than expectation," lives on. To gain ascendency in a society addicted to promises, one must make promises; and yet, since no one can ever satisfy our passion for expectations, he who kindles them is doomed to fail. This accounts for the fickleness for which Americans are notorious. It is a major reason for the periodic throwing-out of the party in power, and for the serial marriage pattern that our social commentators detect is replacing the illusion of monogamy.

Expectations from technology

Another complication is that people have seen massive advances made in those aspects of our system where technology is the key.

Automation, using the new electronic techniques, has multiplied the output of our industrial cornucopia. Computers handle great masses of information and records that would have inundated human capacities. The output of our farms has been increased vastly by machines. But people expect the same multiplications of capabilities where *human* capacities are still the key, and they vent their ire when massive human resources are not available.

The process of teaching cannot be revolutionized by installing automated equipment. Health care can't be turned over to great programmed machines, but still depends on the skills and dedication of highly trained doctors and nurses. And our legal system— while it certainly can benefit from updated procedures and record keeping—cannot hope to match the expectations of multiplied capacity that people have seen in the factory and the office.

So Americans inveigh against all these human systems, blinding themselves to these systems' infinite superiority over their predecessors.

The miracles of mechanization have been most evident in industry and business, and many of our industrialists and businessmen have hypnotized themselves. They see only the new holy grail of more and faster production, which must be fed by constantly increasing the public's expectations.

The automated factory and the computerized office lead to programming the layman's mind to expect greater prodigies and to downgrade the miracle model of the current year.

Today's highly trained managers are schooled in the mastery of tangibles. The computer is their prophet, and its testament is quantification. If it can't be counted it can't be measured, and if it can't be measured it doesn't count.

The intangible human attitudes that underlie the malaise of our times make our "scientific" managers uncomfortable because they defy quantification. Yet their prophet says quantify, so the hatreds, jealousies, ambition, cruelties, greed, and other evils that are the moving forces of today's world must be attacked as if they were numerical factors.

chapter 6   The private sector traps itself

THE buildup of unattainable expectations is abetted by the efforts of social activists to eradicate quickly every problem and to satisfy the urgent demands for the unattainable.

The experience of 250,000 previous generations—that there will always be multiple problems and vast gaps in human desires —are brushed aside. The pileup of new programs, and of programs to straighten out and expand on failed programs, has made the strains on the social system far worse.

Then many in government and academia acknowledged that the effort to have government solve all problems through vast appropriations and new bureaus failed. They "acknowledged" that it was up to the private sector—meaning corporations and trade associations—to really solve the problems, with the guidance of the government.

So, many business leaders rushed to prove the omnipotence of the business system. Impressed with their mastery of the electronic systems, they responded to the call for applying their talents and resources to solving the ills of our society.

The corporations and industries have been groping and experimenting, trying to find what to do. With all good intention, they have been falling into the trap of agreeing that all problems can be eliminated if just the right know-how is applied.

In their own businesses they recognize that each change creates new stresses that call for new adjustments; but they have tackled the vastly more complex social problems as if there is a specific finish line to be marked "success."

They have taken on the elimination of human failings as if the failings were "bugs" in an assembly line. For instance, they have assumed the task of job training for the unskilled and the unmotivated. Each time a program is undertaken it whets the people's demands for more, rather than soothes them with appreciation for its achievement; and it cannot be given up, when it is clearly a failure, for fear business will be accused of abandoning the poor.

Since the main cause of most current problems is that expectations of all groups have been built up far beyond attainability, it was predictable that soon business would become the target for charges that it had failed to accomplish everything that everyone had been led to expect.

Its inability to solve problems that grow faster in the public mind than progress ever can has led to business becoming the target for the public's wrath of frustration.

In May 1969 I said in Milwaukee:

. . . now some in government and among impatient theorists are acknowledging that the effort to have government solve all the problems through vast appropriations and ponderous new bureaus has failed. They seem to be acknowledging that it will be up to the private sector—meaning the big corporations—to really solve the problems, with the help of government.

Now we see many leaders of business rushing to prove the omnipotence of the business system. Corporations grope and experiment, trying to find what to do. They are trying to get a handle on these problems that result from the cascade of change and development in our society. . . .

. . . it is predictable that before long castigation for failing to meet these expectations—and those that follow every step of progress—will be leveled at business.

We may soon find the business community under the most severe attack in its history, because it has been maneuvered into seeming to promise the early solution to ongoing problems.

The months since then have been marked by a Niagara of attacks on business' social failures. Not only in matters of the environment, where their vulnerability is evident, but in all the gamut of people's complaints, business and industry are under a barrage of assaults. So long as they try to meet it by conveying the impression they will solve the problems, they will be flagellated with their own good intentions.

The expectations of employees have raised wages and benefits dangerously beyond the point where much of American industry cannot compete in the world. Expectations of a constantly growing bounty of goodies and gratifications for everyone have been made an intractable part of the American psyche. And the expectation that our problems (this era's replacements for those that have always beset humankind and the forerunners of those that will follow) will be solved by our master managers assures that management will be the hate object of the public's frustrations.

By weaving unrealistic hopes both for what it can produce and for what it can solve, business in America has been in danger of creating its own breakdown.

Fortunately, management groups recently have shown a more realistic approach to coping with the public's attitudes and expectations. Both the new Business Roundtable of industry leaders and the U.S. Chamber of Commerce's Task Force on the Powell Amendment have set broader dimensions for their functions, dealing both with the realities of the problems and the understanding of them by the public. If their guidance is sound, they may avert the growing crisis.

chapter 7 The changed nature of change

IN all previous eras, changes—even man-made changes—tended to come one or a few at a time. They could be evaluated on the basis that other existing factors were stable, and decisions could be reached about each new one that arose. The problem-solving process was still essentially two-dimensional.

A businessman in the latter part of the 19th century could decide to locate a factory in a town that would be served by a new railroad with the reasonable knowledge of what changes would be occurring: what the transportation network availability would be, where new population centers were likely to arise, the sources and approximate cost of raw materials, where and how he would obtain manpower.

When mankind was still almost dependent on unbridled forces of nature, whatever we tried was likely to be a good risk. Some percentage of our efforts were improvements, and the consequences of a failure were slight because the degree of change would be moderate.

While one factor was changing, it could reasonably be expected that the other factors would continue essentially as they had before.

PAST PATTERNS OF CHANGE

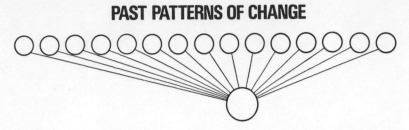

FIGURE 7.1. Old patterns of change, in which one key element was likely to be changing materially at one time. Other elements responded to the alteration of the changing one.

Now new factors and changes arise in multiples. Since almost every element is changing, there are a number of apparently unrelated trends shaping up at any given time. All of these affect existing factors and each other.

The result is that the scope of challenges is multidimensional. They are interrelated, so there are many fronts to be coped with at the same time.

Consequently, the range of factors that are creating new challenges is becoming too diffused to be attacked in a unilateral or even two-dimensional manner.

In our electronically unstabilized existence, the cascade of changes and adjustments is constantly speeded up.

Our sense of balance, based on a long heritage of change occurring at an imperceptible rate, is upset.

Just as if the balance mechanisms of our inner ears were spun about like tops, we are in danger of becoming dizzy and unable to tell in what direction we are headed.

Accordingly, it is necessary to strive for orientation and to take a systems approach to analyzing the problems and to coping with them.

Plans for instituting any change must incorporate intelligent readings on the sequence of interrelated factors, not only of what

PRESENT PATTERNS OF CHANGE

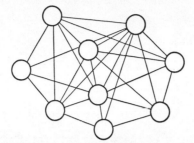

FIGURE 7.2. New patterns of change, in which many elements are changing at the same time, and all are influencing each other's changes.

effects that change will have on other factors, but also what changes will be occurring in those factors for various other reasons, and how they, in turn, will affect the factor under consideration.

A rule of all present-day management is: Every element affects every other element.

Particularly in human-climate areas, countless organizations still approach their situations as if they were unilateral. For instance, they adopt new employment policies without analyzing how they will be affected by changes going on in housing patterns in the area, transportation, school policies, social welfare programs, and many other related factors.

To deal with any factor and reach judgments on what to do with it, it is necessary to analyze and plan for the complexities in which it is involved. There are no isolated considerations, only complex interplays of considerations.

chapter 8 Crucial intangibles in a world of tangibles[1]

ONE axiom of business today on which almost all managers agree is that the job of the good manager is to review all the facts and eliminate as many uncertainties as possible in reaching decisions.

This also describes the function of the computer. Managers add experience and judgment, but the fact-analyzing and uncertainty-eliminating functions are their marks as professionals. Our most admired managers are often described as having computer minds.

These skills aim directly at the classical problem in business: getting to the core of a maze of facts and factors to reach the soundest decision. On the premise that all factors are either knowable or predictable, the professional manager has been trained to concentrate on the facts. He feels he must resist being influenced by the intangibles that will not lend themselves to factual analysis.

The ambitious and discerning younger executive soon learns he will be commended if his programs "stick to specifics," and if his reports are focused on "measurable results." Anything else tends to seem extraneous and may mark him as being "fuzzy" in his thinking. His boss not only responds to this approach but congratulates himself on developing an effective assistant. The assistant, thus trained, becomes the scientific manager of the future.

The excellent managers of this type have achieved awesome mastery of the tangibles of business: production techniques, purchasing, inventory, warehousing, transportation, cost controls, engineering, finance, manpower requirements, and others. The efficiency of production, operations, transportation, and distribution in American business is the envy of most of the world.

The real problems

But the major problems facing business today are mostly intangible, immeasurable, and not subject to factual analysis.

- The main problem in production is no longer increasing the efficiency of our plants, but the attitudes of the people whose jobs are to be changed or eliminated by more efficient methods.

- The principal problem of growth through innovation is not organizing and administering development programs, but the reactions of the intended customers and dealers to the product.

- The personnel problem is not projecting a firm's manpower needs and standards, but persuading the best people to work for the company—and then to stay and do their best work.

- The financing problem is not financial planning for the company's funding, but the attitude of the stock market or other investors.

- The problem in advertising is not minutely analyzing the media, the timing, and the costs, but how to reach the minds and hearts of the audience.

- The problem of business acceptance is not only demonstrating that it operates in the public interest, but getting people to understand that its cornucopia works better when it has a minimum of restraints.

All of these problems, and others, are in the minds of men—the most intangible, immeasurable, and unpredictable of all elements affecting a business.

It is not only that group attitudes are not subject to being fed into computer minds to produce readouts in organized form. Actually, in many cases, the more effort that is made to measure, stabilize, and predict the forces involved in these attitudes, the more wrong the "answers" will be.

The puzzling human

Any one person defies full understanding, as every husband and father (or wife and mother) realizes. We know little about the source of life itself, the forces that carry one through life, or the thousands of thoughts and emotions everyone has every day. Man is just achieving some knowledge of the living virus—an organism incomparably simpler than the simplest of human beings; and the single human being is infinitely simpler than any psychological group to which he belongs. Just one person is a puzzle far greater than any inanimate challenge man has conquered. And a large group of such individuals is vastly more complex than the multiplication of individuals involved.

It is no wonder that group attitudes so far defy the most avid efforts of the fact-minded to classify and control them. It is also not surprising, perhaps, that fact-minded managers tend to bypass those aspects of the total picture that defy their disciplines. And so broad planning and operations are carried on with too little attention to the one factor that will usually determine their success—the attitudes of people.

If only what can be measured is to be considered, then we must ignore the influence in our world of a mother's devotion, a woman's love, a child's admiration, a father's loyalty, joy in the beauty of flowers and music, fun, aspiration, curiosity—in sum, everything that makes life worth living and the world go on.

Applying this to actual decision-making: any computer would have indicated that Britain could not be defended in 1940. Hitler's forces, momentum, and resources were at their apex; and Britain was reeling, without allies and with pitifully thin resources. But Churchill said, "We shall fight on the beaches . . . ," and the intangible human factors of courage, determination, and persuasion made all the "facts" wrong.

The measurable facts originally showed that Truman could not be elected in 1948, and that the United States would not elect a Catholic in 1960. Computers "said" on September 15, 1964, that there was a 95% certainty that the Phillies would win the National League pennant—but then "human psychology" took effect.

Small men sometimes win Olympics medals on spirit; and public attitudes toward the facts of corporate profits, labor relations, and freedom from government interference refuse to respond to the "practical" measures that management uses so well in other problem solving.

The trend in management

It is notable that marketing, which is entirely dependent on the attitudes of dealers and customers—human attitudes—is moving more and more toward computerized thinking. Marketing plans are made that are aimed at making the consumer act as the manufacturer and dealer want him to. But consumers decide that they prefer long-lasting products to obsolescence, and mail- and telephone-ordering to store promotions. And when they get "fed up" with dishonest packaging and come-ons, they ask some branch of the federal government to "protect" their interests.

Many of the recommendations that come out of hard-headed analysis of the "facts" are frustrated by existing attitudes. Not only are the analyses likely to be distorted by the lack of input of attitudes, but the "answers" cannot be executed.

• The railroads' struggle to modernize is stalled by the attitudes of the public and government left over from the roads' old image as ruthless, resulting in undue support for unions' demands and bureaucracies' restrictions.

• When the facts add up to moving a plant or headquarters, the move is often blocked by opposition of employees.

• Growth or improved operations by acquisition or merger increasingly is prevented by the attitudes of the public and government officials, based on fear of concentrated power.

• Efforts to meet threats of new competition are hobbled by resistance of employees: department stores' night and Sunday hours, newspapers' efforts to automate typesetting and use mass-produced ads.

• Need to follow changing social patterns is blocked by lingering prejudices from past problems: efforts of major Illinois banks to follow population trends are balked by the law prohibiting branch banking.

• Efforts to build power plants and refineries needed to meet growing demand for power are frustrated by public opposition to the consequences seen where other such installations have been built, rather than by lack of finances, technology, or skill.

• Meeting unfair competition: the public's readiness to have tax laws favor cooperatives and credit unions over their profit-making competitors.

• Technological innovation: delayed use of new building materials and techniques because legislators cling to old building codes and unions block new methods.

• Building excellence into the staff: employee and community sympathy for the weak but veteran employee; objection of career employees to bringing in outsiders rather than promoting from within.

Using the intangibles

The trend to making everything measure up—therefore, to be measurable—is continuing, however. It is marked by many instances where companies have turned to outside thinkers for answers—and then completely distorted what they offered, in efforts to make it conform to the insistence on tangibility.

• The widely hailed uses of psychology to probe the inner workings of the consumer mind have too often been turned into efforts to manipulate the consumer instead of understand and meet his urges.

• Sociologists' thoughts for coping with social movements tend to be weighed as tools of short-term profit planning.

• Economists hired to probe the dynamics of economic movements and trends have been harnessed to statistics-making for computer programming, to seek predictions of the outcome for specific actions.

• Public relations—which is the overall discipline of understanding, adjusting to, and motivating all group attitudes—is often seen merely as a tool for selling products, like store display or package design.

Where this can lead is seen all too frequently:

- There have been numerous "corporate fads" that rose to prominence because they seemed to offer measurable and visible results. These always include things that can be held, seen, felt, or at least tabulated. A few years ago the community and employee open house was the rage. One could see the 8,000 or 10,000 people go through the plant, drink their Cokes, and look awestruck at the machines. But the costs often were as much as all other public relations budgets for the year; and when few magic transformations of attitude occurred, open houses tapered off to occasional events from which moderate benefits are expected. There was a period when the socko annual report—complete with gatefolds in four colors—was the rage. It, too, could be seen and felt. But costs shot up, stockholders showed little change in attitude, so annual reports are now at a sensible level.

- Projects or budgets are approved on the basis of how tangible they are. One appliance manufacturer spent about $75,000 on one junket for editors because the management could see and talk with them on the trip, thereby sensing it was a "real" activity. A competitor spent a total of $70,000 on a sound (but not-so-visible) public relations program for 12 months, and not only received several times as much favorable press attention but built stature with stockholders, plant communities, dealers, and other publics. Sometimes budget requests of $500 to $2,500 are refused for functions that cannot be felt or handled but are capable of achieving a change in group attitudes; and yet at the same time expenditures of $30,000 to $50,000 are approved for a big meeting complete with floor show.

One trade association that had successfully changed attitudes toward its products over a number of years raised its dues structure substantially, partly to put funds into displays for meetings and literature that could reach only small groups of people. Very meagre additions were made in the budget for the functions that had created the success. But the displays and printed pieces could be seen and felt.

The motive for recommendations

This condition forces those responsible to management to make their recommendations on the basis of tangibility, rather than judgment of actual values. This is the same malady that finds some ambitious men more concerned about their visibility to the boss than about their accomplishments.

These factors apply equally well to marketing management. Great energies have been expended in market research, advertising testing, and audience measurements. Users of these techniques seek to convert the spirit that sparks the human mind into "solid" information; and the social sciences are given respectable status because they may hold promise for codifying the mass human mind.

Advertising then tends to become a numbers game . . . and public relations to become a glorified term for product publicity.

There appears to be a great need for:

1. Realization that the practical-minded man must always make a special effort to seek out the vital factors that cannot be measured and include them in the mix leading to his answers.
2. Awareness of what the intangibles are and their nature.
3. Awareness of their importance in determining the results of any policy, program, or action.
4. Knowing how to direct the course of attitudes—persuade, influence, inform, proselytize, or at least reconcile the people with whom we deal.

These are the ingredients of real public relations. Opinion research, publicity, work with organizations, and the rest are the tools, not the substance, of public relations.

Public relations people of experience and ability are sensitive to these intangible attitudes, know how to sense and test them, and are trained in judgment and techniques for dealing with them. They have a role to play in the total management function.

After all, nothing is more indivisible in a company than its reputation and the climate in which it does business. These are the concerns of the company's public relations, which must be unified as the antenna, the conscience, and the voice of the whole corporation.

Carried to an extreme, efforts to computerize business judgments, in a world run by human attitudes, create their own defeats. They squeeze out the unique and the original, because things or ideas that have not existed before tend to be "vague" and cannot be measured. They solidify the positions of organization men and smother ideas from the outside. They reward the superficial because it can be measured.

Albert Einstein, who is usually considered this century's epitome of the precise, computer-like mind, said, in *Out of My Later Years:* "Perfection of means and confusion of goals seem—in my opinion—to characterize our age."

chapter 9 Contradictions of the critics

ONE of the most crucial facts about the condition of organizations in America is that the spokesmen for our organizations are virtually speechless.

Business and other institutions produce mountains of words that threaten to drown them in paper, yet the overwhelming volume of communication about the workings of our society comes not from our managers but from the intellectual establishment.

While businessmen exchange reports and study projects, the TV and newspaper commentators join with the resident intellectuals on campuses to create the climate of attitudes that shapes most of the changes being imposed on our society.

If the record showed that the intellectuals were also the intelligent segment, and that their wisdom exceeded that of the inarticulate managers, this could be a blessing. Instead, a look at the record demonstrates how serious is the penchant of managers to let themselves be overwhelmed by the rhetoric of the intelligentsia. The untenable logic of many of the manipulations propounded by the intellectual community can be seen in at least two current issues.

For instance, two of the cardinal items of faith among the intellectual communities today are:

1. *The average individual cannot be relied on to assume responsibility for any of his own actions.*

He must have determined for him the type of education he will receive and the number of years of exposure he will have. He should be channelled into a health-care system predetermined by a bureau in Washington and financed with taxes imposed on everyone. He should not be allowed exposure to advertising that some cabal has judged unfit. He should not be allowed to choose a residence characterized by a process of selectivity.

2. *The average individual must be given the power to determine how all our organizations and institutions are operated.*

Illiterates should be given equal voice with the educated in the operation of school systems. Welfare mothers should have as equal a voice in determining tax disbursements as those from whom the taxes are extracted and those who see opportunities to uplift the entire community through the expenditure of the same tax funds. Any individual is encouraged to stop the entire proceedings of a community that is seeking to keep ahead of the needs for housing, power, and other facilities.

These two propositions are propounded by the same intellectual community, which fails to recognize that the two concepts directly contradict each other. When it suits the intellectuals' purpose, people are assumed to be incapable of making any judgments of their own; for another purpose, the demand is that these same people be given the right to impose their judgments on the entire community.

Conflict of freedoms

This contradiction is hardly isolated. The same group of intellectuals generally is ardent in opposing any form of censorship of written and filmed material. They point out that it is tyranny to deny free choice of ideas and entertainment to the many in order to shelter the susceptible few. Though many of them abhor the extreme pornography appearing in many movie theaters, book stores, and magazines, they fight valiantly against censorship lest that principle be carried over to restrain films and literature of other sorts.

They detect the threatening shadow of government control of communications in the pointed urgings of administration executives that the media be coaxed into showing a greater degree of "responsibility" and a broader spectrum of social philosophy.

They feel that Daniel Ellsberg was a hero for stealing classified information on the Vietnam war debates and getting them published.

At the same time, they advocate rigid censorship of what can be said or shown in advertising of products and services by business, in order to shelter the gullible or careless few.

While they deny that the normal individual can be motivated to follow the examples of explicit pornographic depiction, they propose straightjackets be put on legitimate businesses for fear that someone may be motivated to buy a product for reasons other than clear and immediate necessity.

While they insist that all information in government files must be subject to removal and broad publication, as in the case of the Pentagon Papers, they assert their alarm that certain information in government data banks might from time to time be revealed to law-enforcement agencies that are trying to give the innocent citizen a better chance of coping with criminals.

It is serious enough that such inconsistent advocacy goes unchallenged in the power centers where the shape of our society is formed. It is equally serious that the private segment of society that has most to lose from the adoption of many of the advocated policies is tongue-tied and inarticulate.

Before he became a Supreme Court Justice, Lewis F. Powell wrote a timely memorandum titled "Attack on American Free Enterprise System." In it he made this point:

The painfully sad truth is that business, including the boards of directors and the top executives of corporations great and small and business organizations at all levels, often have responded—if at all—by appeasement, ineptitude, and ignoring the problem [of attacks]. There are, of course, many exceptions to this sweeping generalization. But the net effect of such response as has been made is scarcely visible.

In all fairness, it must be recognized that businessmen have not been trained or equipped to conduct guerrilla warfare with those who propagandize against the system, seeking insidiously and constantly to sabotage it. The traditional role of business executives has been to manage, to produce, to sell, to create jobs, to make profits, to improve the standard of living, to be community leaders, to serve on charitable and educational boards, and generally to be good citizens. They have performed these tasks very well indeed.

But they have shown little stomach for hard-nose contest with their critics, and little skills in effective intellectual and philosophical debate.

chapter 10 Government by repression

THERE are several predominant trends in American society today:

1. Burgeoning of diversity, with new fields of endeavor and areas of knowledge proliferating.
2. Great, rapid, and multiple changes in almost all aspects of society.
3. Emergence of larger and more complex organizations, with divisions and subsidiaries related and yet operating largely separate from each other like the heads of Hydra.
4. Rapid internationalization, which multiplies the number of factors that must be known and considered by many managers in operating their organizations.

These conditions add up to one of the most significant trends within our institutional structures: the establishment of teams of managers to run them.

The "Office of the President" concept is one form.

The "Task Force" concept—in which a group of specialists in all necessary disciplines is assembled for a purpose and then disbanded when the purpose has been met—is another.

Yet despite these dynamics that are clearly making it more and more difficult for even the most informed and most professional manager to operate his organization, more and more controls are being imposed by those who not only are unable to know the fields they regulate but are themselves imbedded in massive and turgid organizations.

Despite the growing evidence that controllers in government are becoming less and less efficient in their roles, their bureaucracies continue to grow. Bureaucracies must have functions to justify themselves, and they must appear knowledgeable and authoritative.

So the complexity of almost every field of endeavor is accompanied by a greater complex of controls and dictates from a distant and inexpert coterie of government officials. As President Eisenhower said: "Farming looks mighty easy when your plow is a pencil and you're a thousand miles from the cornfield."

As a result, hundreds of thousands of executives and professional people face growing bafflement. They know how complex their roles are and often feel mounting frustrations over the demands of just keeping up. Yet at the same time they are being harrassed by others who don't know, and seem not to consider, the position and problems of private organizations.

Lewis F. Powell, before he became a justice of the Supreme Court, said in his memorandum:

> Politicians reflect what they believe to be the majority views of their constituents. It is thus evident that most politicians are making the judgment that the public has little sympathy for the businessman or his viewpoint.
>
> American business [is] "plainly in trouble"; the response to the wide range of critics has been ineffective, and has included appeasement; the time has come—indeed, it is long overdue—for the wisdom, ingenuity, and resources of American business to be marshalled against those who would destroy it.

The fact is that businessmen and other private individuals are increasingly losing touch with the sources of control that are being exerted over their operations. Accordingly, learning how to attain influence over these sources and having a role in their determinations have become top priorities for nearly every organization.

In the next chapter we shall see how the patterns of influence have been changing, and private managers are being left behind.

SECTION II The new dynamics of power

chapter 11 Shift in influence patterns

SUPPOSEDLY classless America has long been fascinated by the question of which segment of the populace *really* determines events.

In Colonial times, Jefferson was convinced that it must be the landowners or farmers who produced the "real" needs of society, while Hamilton was sure it must be the merchants and financiers.

The emphasis and identity of the centers of power have shifted through the years. Today there are at least six distinct elements that are presumed by substantial groups to have the real powers of decision:

1. *Big Business.* Advocates of this concept conceive of Big Business as a tight conspiracy acting in unison to assume control over government, labor, education, the church, colleges, and especially "the people." The undeniable powers of business are not seen as a consequence of its size and essentiality to society; nor is the intense disagreement and infighting within the business community taken into account.

2. *The Aristocracy,* usually identified as "The Eastern Establishment." Concentration of finance and communication, the Ivy League colleges, and the federal government in the Boston-

56

New York-Philadelphia-Washington corridor continues to convince many that that is the axis of American power, despite population shifts and the fact that four of our last five presidents came from west of the Mississippi (and the losing candidates in the last six elections were also from the West).

3. *Big Labor.*   When all railroads or long-distance telephone lines shut down, despite pleas and exhortations from the White House, the cry arises that no one dares interfere with the unions, least of all Congress.

4. *The Roosevelt "Coalition."*   Though results of the last two Presidential elections seem to leave this combine of labor-blacks-Catholics-Jews-intellectuals in disarray, there is still support for the concept that this "coalition" is not dead, but is just taking over the Republican Party too.

5. *Big Technology.*   Though there is considerable difficulty in transmogrifying technology into a group of humans who "run things," considerable effort is being made to do so by ecologists and those concerned about self-fulfillment of the individual. The charge that technology is now the ruling force in America—and out of control—has many vocal adherents. By transference, those who finance and operate technological operations are presumed to be the moving forces in society.

6. *Opinion Leaders.*   The most sophisticated concept of a center of influence that directs our lives arises from the concept developed in 1948 by Paul F. Lazarsfeld, Bernard Berelson, and Hazel Gaudet in *The People's Choice.* They propounded that the real centers of influence are scattered throughout society; that the opinion leaders on various issues may be different individuals in any community, and that they tend to be those who most closely follow the mass media. The vast dispersal and the changing identity of opinion leaders on various questions made them most difficult to identify, so the media that are presumed to guide them have come to assume the mantle of opinion leadership.

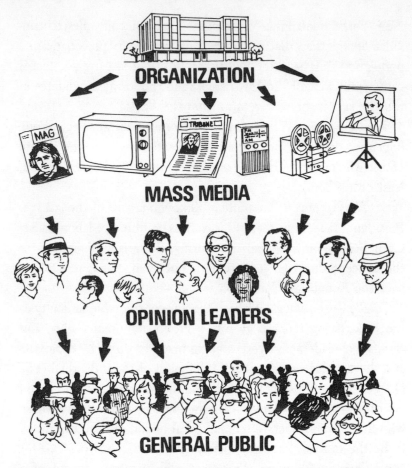

FIGURE 11.1. The traditional concept of how opinion "flows" from the source through the mass media to "opinion leaders" who influence the general public.

Among sophisticated professionals in mass influence, the existence of a group of opinion leaders who pilot the course our society takes has become nearly an article of faith. Figure 11.1 shows how the concept looks in graphic form.

Each of these conceptions of where centers of control exist has an element of truth, yet it requires little study to establish that none of them is actually in control of our society in the way, for instance, the Oxford-Cambridge alumni are in charge in Britain.

Like almost everything else, the concepts of social dynamics have lost their simplicity. The straight-line concept of a controlling group wielding its will on our institutions and all the people is as lost as our innocence. Anyone sitting in the meetings of any of the groups supposed to have such control would recognize that they spend more time discussing their frustrations than celebrating their powers.

A new pattern of influence

It is now apparent that a new pattern of influence has emerged in America that has not yet been recognized. The sense of chaos and impotence that runs through almost all elements of the populace reflects not only frustrations from failures of their aspirations; it reflects also an absence of assurance as to what the "target" really is—where response can be expected to come from. Since the first step in attacking any problem is to understand it, to recognize its nature, let us attempt to do that.

From the standpoint of business, the forces that will shape the future may be categorized into two types:

1. Those that are carried on without systematic control—moved by human actions, but with the consequences almost independent of conscious human direction. These include the changes resulting from thousands of separate decisions and actions in science and technology: new sources of energy, new machines, new medical discoveries, genetic manipulation.

Though there is no framework of control that makes up a system of "Big Technology," the *composite* of what is going on in thousands of laboratories and research centers adds up to an awesome force for change not only in living styles but in attitudes.

It is against this amorphous but potent force that much of the outcry against technology is directed. There are definite signs of human attitudes being shaped to interpose controls on the impact of the science-technology spectrum. The Sierra Club is now a sophisticated attitude-shaping organization. Almost every community has its groups opposed to new power plants, extension of atomic energy, highways to accommodate added outpourings of the automobile factories, airports, and other extensions of technology. It seems to be just a matter of time before such organizations systematically seek to block laboratory work in genetic engineering.

2. Those that are distinctly under human control—the changes resulting from conscious decisions made by persons with the power to take actions affecting people and organizations.

These persons can be defined as the Power Leaders. They are the men and women who are in a position to effect change or exert control *directly* on the freedom, the activities, and the aspirations of many others.

This type of power goes beyond that of the business tycoon. Many business executives have the power to affect directly the lives of some: their employees, the communities in which they operate plants, sometimes the economic conditions throughout segments of enterprise and of the economy. But increasingly that power is being made subservient to the power of coercion from the Power Leaders—the forces in government who pass laws, enact taxes, institute investigations, issue regulations, impose penalties.

Theoretically, the ultimate powers have long resided among the group imbued with the force of law. However, the historic concept that "that government is best that governs least" tended to leave the powers of government as a *corrective* force, rather than one based on initiating mandatory practices and concepts; and private interests continued to be given the priority of privilege both in government practice and public opinion.

The Sherman Anti-Trust Act, the Pure Food and Drug Laws, the Robinson-Patman Act, and others arose in response to crests of criticism, but then tended to subside into disuse. The Securities and Exchange Commission, the Interstate Commerce Commission, the Federal Trade Commission, and other regulatory bodies sank into lethargy and self-perpetuation. In some cases, such as the ICC, the result became more a labyrinthine bureaucracy than assertion of the powers intended by law.

The flow of influence

Recent developments in the dynamics of our society have had significance that is not generally recognized. Most important is a major shift in the pattern of how influence is exerted and how economic and social changes are brought about.

The focal center of action is the group of Power Leaders:

1. *Congress,* with its power to legislate and create new forces to impose on business and the public, such as minority hiring, pollution controls, price and wage controls.

2. *The federal administration,* with its powers to press for legislation, select which legislation to really activate, determine the manpower and character of the courts and the regulatory agencies.

3. *The courts,* with their powers to interpret laws "creatively" or "strictly."

4. *Regulatory bodies*—such as the Department of Justice, the FTC, the ICC, the FCC, the Office of Price Stabilization, the Food and Drug Administration—with their powers to impose limits on many aspects of business' and the public's functions.

5. *The state and local counterparts* of these federal powers.

But to say that the powers of direction lie with these Power Leaders would be to oversimplify.

It is the *nature* of the forces that bring these powers to take their actions that is crucial and largely unrecognized. New cir-

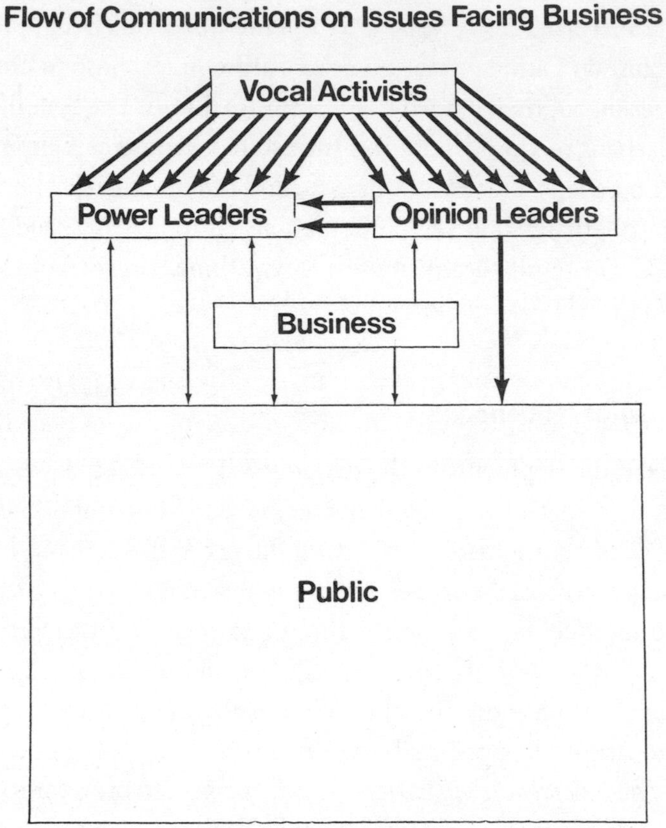

Flow of Communications on Issues Facing Business

FIGURE 11.2. Schematic diagram of how influence tends to move today. Vocal activists influence the attitudes of opinion leaders much more than do other segments, including business. Together, vocal activists and opinion leaders have predominant impact on the Power Leaders—those who can take action to change society (Congress, the federal administration, regulatory agencies, state and local government, the courts).

cumstances forestall the old pattern of having new laws and regulatory bodies fade into impotence or get snarled in red tape after they are enacted.

Today, the pattern of influence in the United States looks like that shown in Figure 11.2.

It can be seen that the Power Leaders are the target of heavy input from the articulate opinion leaders—the media and educators—and from the newly emerged vocal activists such as Ralph Nader, the ecologists, advocates of welfarism, and others. These inputs are, indeed, far more concentrated and intensive than the input the Power Leaders receive from either business or the general public.

In this unbalanced situation, it is not surprising that far greater credence is given to the visible and aggressive inputs than their true representation of the public's concern warrants. It also creates a far greater sensitivity to those expressions that are received from the general public than their seriousness warrants.

• In one instance, massive headlines for a simplistic "expose" were accompanied by strong efforts by activist groups to "get the mail in" to Congress. By best estimates, 80,000 letters were received—about half of them refuting the accusations or neutral. The negative mail, despite the efforts of the activists, amounted to about 1/16 of 1 percent of the supposedly affected populace. Yet in the climate of alarm created by the activists and the media, Congress and the affected agencies reacted as if a dire crisis of public confidence had occurred.

Even in a Republican administration noted for its friendliness to business, the effect of this activist-media saturation impact on the Power Leaders has been notable. Agencies once derided for their quiescence have moved to an activist stance.

a.   The National Transportation Safety Board has scalded general aircraft manufacturers, the railroads, and the auto manufacturers.
b.   The Department of Justice has pressed antitrust actions against IBM and Consolidated Foods.

c.   The FTC has pursued a new doctrine of "corrective" advertising.

d.   The FDA has given notice of its intention to ban hundreds of drugs, to rule heavily vitamin-fortified foods off the shelves, and to require nutritional-content labeling.

e.   Even the Federal Communications Commission—dealing with the supposedly powerful broadcast media—has begun to challenge relicense applications.

Differences among "opinion leaders"

The once amorphous group of "opinion leaders" now can be seen as three rather distinctive segments:

1.   The articulate purveyors of information and ideas—the media and educators.

2.   The vocal activists who exploit the media and the arts of sensation to make their causes visible.

3.   The Power Leaders.

These three groups form nearly a closed loop of communication, as seen in Figure 11.2. The activists and the media need and use each other, and both exert far more impact on the Power Leaders than the vast mass of the public or any private institutions, including business.

It is no secret that Congress, the White House, the federal courts, and the regulatory agencies are all increasingly out of touch with the public and business. Awareness of this gulf is expressed often by government officials and commentators who observe the Washington scene.

This gulf is fostered by the continuing preference of most of the business community for low-key, low-profile, traditional communications methods.

The primary tactic of some big corporations and some trade

associations has been to exert influence on government officials in private. This takes the form, legitimately, of supporting their election efforts (through personal donations and executives' work in fund raising) and meeting with them to propound their cases; and occasionally, illegitimately, of arm twisting and proferring favors. Now, however, this unilateral, confidential type of input is being made more visible by greater spotlighting of financial contributions (from the ITT contribution for the Republican convention fund to legal requirements that all contributions be publicly revealed) and by the probing of the Ralph Naders, the Jack Andersons, and the iconoclastic staff people within government and business.

At the same time, the personal influence of those opposed to business—professional consumerists, minority-organization leaders, ecologists, militant women's groups, and others—has been stepped up and, together with labor, offsets the strength of the inner-circle inputs of business spokesmen.

The strong impact of their mass-media efforts on the Power Leaders is making the trickle of such communications from the private sector a whisper in a windstorm.

We can conclude that:

1. There has been a critical shift in the pattern of how influence is exerted in our society, and how economic and social changes are being brought about.

2. Indications are that this pattern will be accentuated, rather than fade.

3. Business and other parts of the private sector have become the object of changes originating with groups inimical to their interests, in the name of the public that these groups do not truly represent.

4. The private sector, being long established and having a sense of entrenched security, continues to function as though conditions had not changed. While its voice is overwhelmed in

the halls of the Power Leaders and its existence is being reshaped as a result, business expends perhaps 1/6 of 1 percent of its volume on direct and indirect input to the Power Leaders (about $1.15 billion spent on nonproduct communications and public relations). It spends about 17 times that much on traditional advertising to sell its products—much of it giving fuel to the vocal activists for their attacks on business.

chapter 12 The "smart bombs" of dissent

Most established organizations have traditionally maintained a "low profile" and kept their operations private.

Throughout the half century between 1920 and 1970, the craft of public relations flowered profusely. The overwhelming majority of communications efforts dealt with those aspects of the organization's functions that the management could benefit from having the public know.

There was extensive product publicity, open houses to show off sparkling new facilities, films and literature that projected the organization's image as a progressive "good citizen" of industry and the community, "message" publicity about the importance of an industry in creating jobs or the inadvisability of some given legislative or regulatory proposal, and the like.

Those managers who emerged into public view did so usually in connection with advisory bodies, propounding of economic doctrines, contributions to universities and health organizations, and the like.

Still, it was considered unseemly for an executive to seek public view. It was a common rule in many organizations that the chief executive's public appearances should never, except in times of

The people factor: Managing the human climate

dire emergency, number more than two a year. This also reflected concern about upsetting any groups that might take issue with the views expressed.

There was a transition from the entrepreneur-executive such as Henry Ford I and John D. Rockefeller to the professional manager who advanced to chief executive for a few years' tenure before retirement. This pattern submerged the identity of business leaders.

There arose the specter of antitrust action and the suspicion that the controllers in Washington were more likely to take after an organization that seemed conspicuous. That also contributed to the traditional wisdom among private organizations that, while the times had made the vest largely obsolete, it was still wise to play one's cards very close to it.

So it has come as a shock to many managers to find that the "low profile" exposes them where they are most vulnerable.

The new activist-media force that has risen to prominence in the last few years is the "smart bomb" of our modern social system. It is able to seek out and attack what were previously low-profile organizations and institutions.

Critics take over initiative

The initiative in determining which organizations will have the spotlight on them has been yanked out of the hands of the leaders of the organizations and taken over by the aggressive and vocal militants among public groups and the communications industry.

Some of the most comfortable havens have felt the blasts: not only business, but universities, foundations, churches, the law, medicine, unions—and even the media themselves. Companies and industries that had kept their roles quietly behind the scenes are among the most attacked today.

For years the pharmaceutical manufacturers basked in the devotion accorded them by a public that appreciated the new "miracle drugs." They reveled quietly in the benefits of esteem and high profits. The attacks on them came suddenly and left many managers in the industry incredulous that such an assault could happen to them.

The American Telephone and Telegraph Company was the haloed friend of widows and orphans, the prime example of the well-managed large organization, the dedicated institution that connected everyone with everyone else in the outside world at nominal monthly rates. When the attacks came in multiples over breakdowns in service in New York, questioning of special charges for nonstandard equipment, employment practices, and other issues, the ramparts of AT&T's fortress proved porous indeed.

The oil drillers benefited from virtual invisibility because of the remoteness of their sites. The economy moved on automobile wheels that were driven by their petroleum. Power and warmth were provided by the wells they drilled. Hardly any profile could be lower (except in remote outposts where derricks reached skyward) than that of the petroleum drilling industry. Yet the critics have laid down a formidable barrage on depletion allowances, oil spills in offshore sites, tax allowances, and various other accusations.

For many years, countless executives went home each evening secure in the anonymity and unquestioned authority that a low profile afforded them. Now a low profile indicates secretiveness, and in today's human climate the impression of secretiveness breeds distrust.

chapter 13   The evolution of leaders

IN most areas of endeavor, the process of replacement has constantly outrun the ability of the old to renew. Men or women eminently suited to one era often are rendered obsolete by the next, because they do not adapt themselves to new patterns.

In just the past six generations in America, we have seen perhaps seven successive cycles of dominant types of men.

Those who settled the virgin areas were individualistic farmers, frontiersmen, craftsmen. Though the American genius for working things out together when stress demanded was becoming evident, individualism was the cherished trait. Most men thought little of what others felt about them. They were suspicious of learning and polish.

Then came the tinkerer who invented or adapted, creating things that filled or developed new needs.

He became or gave rise to the entrepreneur, the early builder of organizations and systems.

There followed the opportunist, the plunging, gambling "robber baron" who took advantage of the chartless new social climate to build and accumulate.

Then arose the master salesman who found ways to market the growing outputs of the big enterprises using the more complex systems. Large and widespread enterprises they built displaced the craftsman and the scarcity-oriented entrepreneur.

As the enterprises got bigger and the social climate exerted restraints, the way was opened for the lawyer, the angle-player, the lobbyist.

Then came the financial men, who through their mastery of building with other people's money converted enterprises from monarchies into uneasy republics.

And now we are seeing the ascendency of men trained to manage complex and multifaceted organizations—hybrids who succeed in relation to how well they can encompass the scope and intricacy of hydra-headed operations.

It is clear that the times determine the ascendency of various traits. The nature of the social milieu creates the needs for talents and personality. Those who sense the needs and best adapt themselves have most often gained the rewards.

Today the emerging need is clearly for the man who combines skill in managing complex structures with sensitivity and knowledge about the vital human climate.

As we shall see in the next chapter, there are major additional forces that now influence the source and nature of the newest generation of managers. Since every organization's future can be no better than the caliber of talent it is able to attract and hold, these forces—and the human climate in which they are arising —are of paramount importance.

chapter 14 The restrictive effects of free choice

Wʜᴀᴛ man has wrought is spinning at a furious rate; but man himself is the great balance wheel, a stabilizing force.

When we explore what might be the limits to acceleration of change—already at a pace where "future shock" is said to ravage us all—that is a key factor that tends to be overlooked.

A force for stability that has received little attention is the evolution of each individual's life span. We all go through a necessary sequence of maturing stages that can be little hurried. Production of a refrigerator may have been speeded up a thousandfold, but production of the human is still scheduled for about nine months. The change of ideas that lead to turmoil may be a thousand times faster than a century ago, but the evolution of the human personality has been only moderately speeded up.

The heritage of the individual and the events he is exposed to combine to bring him to the stages of decision in his life with the inclinations that mold his choices. He makes a choice for the interests he follows, the career he selects, the political and social leanings, the type of friend and lover—all based on how he has been shaped by inheritance and nurture.

This is an age when most people have by far the greatest range of choices that any large populace has ever had. The individual can, with comparatively few restrictions, live where he chooses, associate with whom he pleases, and select the life's work he prefers. Where there appears to be no choice, there is usually a negative choice made. The dropout who avoids social contacts and forgoes career opportunities has also made his choice.

With such a wide range of choice and a wide freedom to choose, it is inevitable that there be a close correlation between those who make the choice and the fields they choose. People are attracted to careers that suit their psyches.

It is important for managers to understand the processes that lead people into various careers and ways of life. Certain types of personality are attracted to a given field, and there is a shaping process involved in preparing someone for it and concentrating on it. Together these tend to instill certain ways of thinking and feeling that help determine what you can expect a person's leanings and responses to be. They have much to do with whether that person can be reached by various types of communication, and how efforts to reach him should be shaped. They also help explain why those in various groups have different outlooks than other people and tend to reshape their observations and opinions in characteristic ways.

New process of selection

Until recently, most young people followed the careers marked for them from birth. They knew they would be farmers or blacksmiths or clergymen, as their fathers were or aspired them to be. Growing up in awareness of what they would become, the career choice shaped them. The farmer-to-be not only was shaped by the rustic life he led but by the pastoral life he foresaw. The predestined clergyman grew up preparing himself for piety. The about-to-be lawyer shaped himself unconsciously to find the role of advocate suitable.

Among the many great changes of our time is a drastic change in this process of the person being shaped by the mandatory career. Today the man or woman seeks the calling, and the calling attracts the individual.

The young person with the sense of free choice seeks out the career that attracts him, by positive intention or negative elimination. If he is repelled by the scramble of competition in the business world, he chooses to teach, to write, to preach, to paint— whichever more cloistered calling seems to offer the most appealing rewards for his talents or traits. In making his choice, he justifies himself by glorifying the field he chooses and reinforces his beginning aversion to business by feeling superior to those who find the business career appealing.

In the same way, of course, the young person who finds the campus, the studio, or the pulpit dull and its rewards too intangible is likely to option for a run at the competitive stakes of business. And he, too, spends a lifetime justifying his choice and feeling superior to those who "chicken out" of the scramble that exhilarates him.

The pill and the economic revolution have doubled the proportion of the population that can freely preselect its career choices. Most girls today can nurture a preference for the kind of work they will do.

Thus we find a process of selection emerging—a selective process that increasingly directs people into walks of life and social strata by considered choice and personal inclination.

A force for stability

It is ironic that a consequence of this liberalization of the person's freedom has become one of the greatest forces for stability and conservatism. In fact, at a time when change in so many aspects of our society has been speeded up to a kaleidoscopic pace, the tendency for people to follow the fields that attract them because of the images they have built over generations actually bolsters the conservative nature of the established professions and callings.

The image of a field is, after all, based on a composite of the traits of those who have entered it through the generations. Each field has acquired an unspoken list of characteristics: mental leanings, bearing and mannerism, even physical appearance.

There are countless exceptions, but there is certainly a vague consensus, for instance, of what a lawyer is supposed to be like— how his mind works, what he seeks from life, how he deports himself, his posture and his presence.

The young person who is attracted by this image of the lawyer comes to associate himself with it. He not only is likely to favor those traits from the start but subconsciously to shape himself to suit them. When he enters law school the whole process intensifies. He has begun with certain inclinations and then has pre-shaped his character and leanings. He comes to associate mostly with other young people who have had the same preshaping and the same general view of the world. He is taught by men and women who went through the same process a generation before and have spent their lifetimes being constantly more sharply honed to their specialties. He is evaluated in terms of how well he meets the measures and expectations of the legal profession— which are the results of generations of refinement and honing.

When he gets his law degree, he is likely to spend the rest of his working life—and much of his free time—associating with lawyers, the law, and jurists.

Even while all other fields grow rapidly more complex and harder for him to understand, the law becomes more complex and requires more of his attention.

So while the cascade of change in the rest of human activities seems to accelerate around him, he is likely to become a stalwart pillar of tradition within the perspective of his chosen field.

The forces of selection

The same process can be seen in virtually every field of long standing. The person who is attracted to medicine is likely to find scientific studies stimulating, to be attracted by prestige and social stature, to appreciate affluence, to enjoy being the object of gratitude for curing disease and even saving life. This preselection of medical students is then honed by the associates he learns with, the teachers who mold him, the societies whose standards he must meet, the codes of ethics, the pattern of practice, the levels of compensation, and the whole mosaic of being a medical practitioner.

Reinforcing the individual's preselection is the selective process of the field itself. The student seeks out the field he identifies with, but the schools in each field also have fine-meshed nets that keep out many of those who might see themselves in the "wrong" light. This is no longer an arbitrary process of screening out ethnic or racial types, but it must continue to screen out the personality that the dons feel would repel the patient or the client; the person who lacks the stamina for sleeping on hospital sofas; the person with poetic leanings who tends to disappear for stretches to commune with his soul while patients suffer.

The person who goes into college teaching, the government official, the social worker, the electrician, the career soldier, the devoted housewife—all tend to be preselected for personality type, to be refined by their associations and teachers, to be measured on scales established by their predecessors.

Considering the force of preselection, as well as the familiar shaping forces of our institutions, it is surprising that we find as much divergence as there is. There are occasional conservative faculty members, socially active businessmen, Dave Meggysseys and Jim Boutons of the sports world, the Michael Crichtons and Somerset Maughams who abandon medicine for literature, an Armand Hammer who never used his M.D. but became an international oil magnate.

The process of solidifying within each field may be accelerating.

As the range of career opportunities multiplies and each field becomes more complex and demanding to learn, the individual is likely to be really familiar with few of them. Schools are abandoning the attempt to give each child an ample taste of many potential career fields. Children are choosing their bents earlier and committing themselves—not to actual careers, but to psychological leanings that will lead them to career choices.

A new source of conflict

The conflict between the conservatism of various fields and the mounting pressure on all fields to change may be one of our next sources of turmoil.

Our already rapidly changing society is being exhorted from many sides to change even faster. In our present age of activism, everyone seems to feel he knows how to manage everyone else's field though he feels uncertainty about staying abreast of his own.

Every career area is being pressured by others to revolutionize itself to "achieve" the others' imposed goals.

College faculties are under duress from administrators, legislators, industrialists, students, conservatives, radicals, clergymen, and the media. Most of these demand nothing less than that professors who have been inclined toward their way of performing since puberty must overnight become just the opposite type of person.

Politicians who go through the periodic hell of all-or-nothing elections because they seek the headiness of power are told by groups who enjoy the security of tenure that they must become selfless servants, following the dictates of every conflicting desire.

Doctors who entered medicine for prestige, independence, and money are told by groups outside of medicine they must become salaried employees like supermarket butchers and bank tellers.

Businessmen who chose the competitive sphere because they feel the zest to manage and make decisions are castigated if they do not become passive sifters of others' input, mere gatekeepers of multiple directives on how they must operate their businesses.

People who have rejected careers involving discipline and making complex organizations work, insist on telling managers how to manage: college faculties to presidents, government bureaucrats to business managers.

In most cases the motives seem admirable, but blindness to what is attainable is marked.

We all feel the urgency to bring about change—except in our own spheres.

Journalists no longer only report events, but press all our institutions to transform themselves—except how they themselves prepare their newspapers, broadcasts, magazines, or journals.

Professors vilify every element of our society for not transforming itself as their wisdom dictates—except how they teach (or strive to avoid having to teach).

Ministers use their pulpits to define how cities, institutions, professions must be reshaped—but resist any real changes in the centuries-old tenure of the ecclesiastics.

Reconciling opposite forces

We are faced with a new and intriguing dilemma: Are the forces that attract people into their chosen spheres strong enough to resist concerted efforts to disembowel them; or will these efforts so distort the various career fields that most of the best prospects will be chased off because the careers will no longer be attractive?

If the latter should happen, what kind of society will result from having all fields largely peopled by practitioners who are inclined in the opposite direction from their purposes?

How many properly endowed young people will be attracted into college teaching, government service, business management, medicine, and other demanding careers requiring many years of sacrifice, if the traditional appeals of these careers are obliterated?

The dilemma is creating a new range of human relationships. It creates the need for the "review board" that oversees a career field but does not seek to impose hamstrings on it.

It is startling but meaningful that one of the first of these review boards is a group of respected nonmembers of the journalistic profession organized into a board to review practices of the information media—long the field most immune from criticism.

The delicacy and finesse required to oversee without overruling are traits that we have not yet learned, and that few are prepared for. Most ventures in this direction have been signally unimpressive, either overregulating their fields into torpor, such as the Interstate Commerce Commission's deathlike hand on the railroads, or failing to exert any real direction, such as the Department of Labor.

It is now clear that the military must be subject to the constant review of civilians. More than ever, the processes of preselection and fine honing are making military men different in outlook and inclination from the rest of society.

Similarly, there will be growing need for civilian boards to review police, trustees to oversee college faculties and administrations, review bodies for business, evaluation committees for nonprofit organizations and, eventually, nonreligious reviewers of the churches.

But the forces that attract and shape those who can achieve

anything meaningful in our institutions must be kept powerful. The moves to force opposite procedures on all groups and fields while our institutions and entire society rapidly become more complicated threaten to paralyze our system.

Many aspects of our society—the colleges, many government bodies, hundreds of businesses, programs for health and welfare—already show visible loss of vigor because they are buffeted among multiple and irreconcilable outside pressures and cannot function decisively.

This would be serious enough if we were isolated, because growth of our population and its expectations demand vigorous advancement. But it is critical because other societies not facing such emaciation stand ready to move up over our paralyzed form.

While the need for review bodies takes hold and we learn how to make them work, the forces that populate the various career areas and institutions go on, though often blunted and bent. To some, the built-in stabilization of preattraction and self-perpetuation of our institutions that results may seem to be barriers to progress. In the context of how these institutions and our whole society really works, however, this stabilizer seems to be a bulwark of stability and order.

Any manager who considers the human climate in which his organization will function needs to consider the disparate forces that will determine the sources and nature of future personnel, and the conditions under which organizations will be expected to function.

chapter 15 Survival in an age of activism

Two main trends of our society are forming into a classic confrontation. Since it is not likely that either trend will prevail completely over the other, it is likely that this confrontation will bring changes of great importance to every manager.

On one hand, there appears to be an irrepressible growth of large and complex organizations that are needed to provide the vast and multiple requirements of an expanding society.

On the other hand, there are the growing "humanist" attitudes of a mass-educated populace that wants to put the individual beyond the control of any organization or system.

The need for large systems and regimentation of information and control is evident from a quick look at what has been happening to our society.

As we achieve our goal of affluence for almost everyone, the ability to make many buying decisions—rather than just covering the essentials—becomes available to more than 200 million people. With this goes a vast explosion in record keeping and paperwork.

As millions of additional families are able to buy a wide range of products and services other than food, clothing, and shelter, the complex of retailing, wholesaling, distribution, and manufacture multiplies.

The sheer volume of billing and other record keeping expands exponentially. Where a few years ago charge accounts at department stores were the privilege of the top few families, now most families not only have charge accounts at various stores but carry several credit cards, have credit established with banks and finance companies, and have one or more bank accounts.

A generation ago it was pointed out that if the telephone system had not been automated there would not be enough women in the United States to meet the need for telephone operators. So today—even with considerable computerization already accomplished—there are bottlenecks of paper-handling capacity at many points.

Computerization goes all the way back to the source of raw materials and the fabricator of products. And computerization of such complexity favors the large organizations that can benefit from the economy of vast volumes.

Building and operating large organizations is increasingly a matter of huge financing. Large, well-known, and respected organizations have always been able to obtain financing more readily and less expensively than smaller organizations. Recent trends toward large financial institutions dominating the world of finance, with the accompanying decline of the small investor, has further skewed the advantage for the big organization. So while the cost of meeting the latest techniques and technologies goes up sharply, the ability of smaller organizations to finance these needs has become more restricted.

Similarly, the need for major investment to operate efficiently is evident in many other fields. Finding and shipping oil and natural gas, once an attractive lure for the wildcatter operating on a shoestring, is more and more a practice open only to vast organizations. Bids for speculative drilling sites have shot up into millions of dollars per acre. Costs of vast supertankers and pipe-lines can be met only by giant corporations or even combines of giants.

Similarly, the voracious needs for coal require at the start huge drills and immense shovels.

In the production of almost all consumer goods, not only autos but most of our food, the trend toward vast organizations appears to be relentless. The retreat of our agriculture from the family farm to vast agribusiness enterprises has been far faster than any such major social transition in history.

And as enterprises have grown to vast size, so have the services they need—from accounting firms, architects, and law offices to cafeteria catering and office-machine servicing.

To deal with this growth of enterprise, unions have likewise become vast organizations, and the shift of government to keep score and regulate their operations has been strongly toward vast bureaus in Washington.

The opposition of the individual

As relentless as this movement for bigness and inevitable im-personality appears, it would underestimate the strength of the human psyche to predict that the big organization will overwhelm the individual.

As always, here we find the very success of our organizations creating the problems that confound them.

As our system has generally eliminated the constant struggle against shortages and potential disaster, it has liberated the in-dividual from concern about economic necessities.

Most people have assumed that their economic necessities will be met. They focus their concerns on the enrichment of their lives. The stimulus of hunger has been shifted from the necessities to the niceties of living. And almost every individual has a wide range of choice for what he does with his life and what he does with each day.

As a result, fewer and fewer people see the organizations and institutions as vital to their needs, but rather as barriers to their impulses. They have taken for granted the availability of food, shelter, clothing, power, and the other requirements of life that they have found as pervasive as the atmosphere all their lives.

They have developed a vast range of interests and desires, almost all of which were undreamed of just a generation ago. They find it is difficult to achieve many of these aspirations and desires. At each turn in their efforts, they encounter the resistance or the ponderousness of one or more organizations. So they come to view the organization as a repressor of the individual and an enemy of freedom.

It was the large university that suffered the greatest impact of student activism in the late 1960s. It has been the large corporations, for the most part, that have been the targets of the activist assaults on business.

Many of the disenchanted individuals have formed dissent groups and become activist opponents of organizations and system. The organizations are berated both for not meeting all expectations and for organizing into complex systems to try to meet them.

In an age of visibility and communications, the preponderence of those who are antisystem polarize into groups that thrive on visibility and in the communications media. The dissidents who presume that all complex organizations are suspect, if not *prima facie* enemies, cluster into the activist consumer organizations, ecology groups, prominority committees, and other organizations devoted to capturing maximum public visibility. And many of them turn for their careers to the media and "advocacy law," where they feel they can find levers to crack apart the organizations they distrust.

The dissidents write their tracts by electric light, travel to their meetings by automobile, sustain themselves by the produce of the vast agribusiness network, depend on the telephone system operated by the world's largest enterprise, function within educational systems made possible by the funding of big government and big business. Even those who reject our system sufficiently to live in remote communes derive far more of their necessities from the system than from the primitives they try to emulate. Singly or together, they have propounded no reasonable alternative for meeting the needs of a vast advanced society.

Not only the organizations but the people—including the dissidents—who depend on those organizations for virtually all of their needs are in jeopardy.

Finding the means to survive in this activist whiplash calls for the greatest ingenuity in our society. It is a mammoth human-climate challenge.

chapter 16   The mass
production of dissidents

THE number of activist protestors and the number
of causes they espouse are certain to grow. Their expansion is now
built into our system.

The multiplication of the number of people who have received
advanced education has not only created a vast pool of trained
personnel and alert citizens. It has resulted in millions of people
who have been educated to think they should have a special place
in our society.

The college degree has been proffered as a key to being freed
from routine roles in life and as the mark of leadership. Very few
young people who have followed this lure and spent four years
in an atmosphere of such expectation fail to be transformed by
it. The college-educated person is oriented for life to the expectation of special stature, a significant career role, and respect for
his individuality and opinions.

More young people than ever before are achieving stature,
respect, and a choice of lifestyles, yet only a few find they can
attain the rosy expectations that were held out to them, so disillusion sets in.

Those who have been led to expect great things then seek to

justify themselves. They are disappointed with their small roles, and they have the time, the inclination, and the opportunity to attack the structure.

The increased leisure and affluence made possible by the system they attack makes their constant attack on that system possible.

Many of these people spend their time trying to force change in the system they hate for failing to recognize their unique worth. Yet when change comes, it suits only a few because any change can raise but a small percentage of the total to new fulfillment. Both those who have benefited and those who have not then will need new causes to occupy them, since the channels for their energies within the organizational structures can only partly fulfill their dreams.

This makes inevitable the incessant pressure for other changes from a larger and larger segment of the population.

This is a pattern that does not promise to be solved or alleviated by changes, no matter how fast or numerously they may come.

The pressure for change is a force in itself, not to be satiated by the achievement of change.

It now seems certain that the number of dissidents will continue to grow and the number of activist attacks on the system —and on almost every institution in it—will increase in various directions.

For the manager, this inevitably means that much of his time and attention will have to be devoted to the human-climate factors. All other considerations may be meaningless if he cannot operate, or if he must take dictation from outside forces with little interest in the welfare of his organization.

Failure to recognize this might mean turning over more and more of the impetus of the organization to those who are avowed enemies of its objectives.

chapter 17 Prestigious welfare

A "welfare culture" much broader and more insidious than the one that has been exposed as a national dilemma is now spreading throughout our society.

Many of our national, political, and economic policies are now based on providing make-work for millions of supposedly competent people, rather than for those who are left behind by the elimination of menial jobs.

As a result of the drive to provide a major segment of the population with college degrees, there are thousands of liberal arts majors graduated each year, thousands of engineers, thousands of teachers. All of these expect prestigious jobs as their right because, as we have seen, they feel they have been promised to them.

The recession of 1970–71, when thousands of new graduates found no jobs waiting for them, accented the potential for disruption from failing to find niches for these people.

So forces are set up to provide the jobs:

• Government subsidies for space programs, military production, and "think tank" projects that occupy engineers and technicians have become the newest "pork barrel" of government.

• Study groups are formed to explore various issues and proposals with an almost cynical awareness that their reports will serve only to employ their staffs and the office workers who will reproduce and file them.

• Government is unashamedly designated as "the employer of last resort," largely committed to employing personnel who cannot find places elsewhere. Persons employed must then be given assignments in keeping with the nature of their training, so existing bureaus are swelled, and new agencies are formed. All of these need countless secretaries, clerks, administrators, and service personnel.

• Groups devoted to providing social services employ those who majored in social work or fields with no visible outlets for support. These groups develop a stake in the social engineering they are assigned to, so that a solution to the problems faced is among the least desirable of their goals.

• New social-action organizations proliferate as the "causes" develop and as the nuances of their objectives splinter off into the kind of proliferation that has long marked religious sects in this country.

With a growing abundance of teachers, educational philosophy obligingly shifts to justify smaller class sizes, specialists without classrooms, teachers' assistants, and new layers of counselors and administrators.

The acceleration of make-work

Then the pressures of Parkinson's Law are felt increasingly. With more people available, the structure of countless organizations—including many in business—grows to accommodate those people. The functions that are called for proliferate to justify the hours of personnel time that multiply.

Each make-work function creates needs for other "knowledge workers":

a. Bookkeepers and accountants to handle the paperwork of payrolls and time sheets.

b. Clerks and programmers to handle the increase in reports and efficiency studies.

c. Government office workers to handle the paperwork imposed on private organizations in order to inform the government of the extent of employment and the adherence to requirements created to keep the increasing army of government employees busy.

d. Lawyers to write laws that will inject the government's force into more areas of private activity, and more lawyers that the private organizations need to cope with them.

e. Enlarged personnel staffs to employ the additional clerical and bookkeeping help made necessary by the make-work practices and to keep records on the staff people who previously were unnecessary.

The proliferation of those filling positions that were previously unnecessary extends into almost every area. Political scientists have to create programs to experiment with, so study projects are funded and staffed. People who are put on various payrolls as researchers to conduct such study projects need funds, aides, secretaries, and clerical personnel.

All of this creates more paperwork that needs more paperworkers, who create jobs for bookkeepers and clerks, who in turn require supervisors and administrators drawn from the supply of educated people. Here is a self-powered spiral that has defied all efforts to arrest it.

Millions think they are doing important work, but they are really only shuffling each other's papers and creating "needs" for each other to meet. This is massive make-work for the educated, or prestigious welfare.

A large proportion of the national economy has become dependent on this mass-production of nonproductivity.

Millions of square feet of the office buildings that have brought prosperity to the construction trades and jobs to thousands of workers are occupied by the millions on prestigious welfare. Much of the economy of the manufacturers of building materials, of office machines and supplies, of furniture and telephones is devoted to meeting the needs of this group.

Much of the burden of this is unavoidable to an organization's management. It must meet the voracious demands of those employed in government, such as multiple voluminous reports, tax records, and the like. The demands imposed by the make-work in government are beyond a manager's control. But much of it is controllable within the manager's organization if he is aware that the pressure of the spiral exists and that the number of people employed is a poor index of the effectiveness and scope of an organization.

chapter 18   The ephemeral nature of youth

Much of the turbulence in our human climate originates with youth.

Our young people are most sensitive to new currents of thought. Their scope of experience is narrow, so what has occurred in the last few years assumes much greater importance proportionately than it does to those who have experienced a much broader scope.

Youth also has the fewest anchors to established ways or systems.

Few of them are really aware of what their parents do for a living.

They have very little understanding of how any of our organizations or institutions function or the problems they must deal with.

They have few roots, in an age when it is likely their fathers have changed jobs several times since they were born, and they have moved from city to city.

They have little concern for the problems of making a living, in this era when having more than the necessities has been taken for granted.

And they have very little loyalty invested in any system or

organization, as evidenced by the much thinner veneer of attachment to their schools than was traditional with previous generations.

With its sensitivity to new currents of thought and with few ties to existing structures, youth turns readily with the winds of change. While it is impossible to predict what the new pressures of youth will be, it is certain that they will not be the same as they are today or have been in the past.

The focus of youth's agitation has shifted approximately every two years since 1960:

a. Activism for blacks—the "freedom marches" and the sit-downs in public places.
b. Freedom from administrative authority—takeovers of the campuses at Berkeley and Columbia, vandalism of buildings, "free speech" gambits.
c. The Vietnam war—peace marches, protest demonstrations, destruction of R.O.T.C. buildings.
d. "The system"—bombings of computer centers, attacks on campus recruiters from big businesses.
e. Ecology—Earth Day, organized opposition to new power plants and highways.
f. The "Jesus revolution"—group religious experience, organized conversions, visible self-abnegation.
g. Self-interest—concern for school work, attention to career goals, popularity of stereo sets and cars.

Every thrust of the youth culture is vitiated as soon as it becomes "in" long enough to be identified with one age group.

The generation gap used to be between fathers and sons; it now appears to be between younger and older brothers or sisters.

The concerns and interests of youth are important to managers not only because of the potent impact that youth itself has come to have in recent years. They also are important because they set up waves that surge through society as a whole, reducing in impact as they reach the outer edges but still having their effects on the attitudes and preferences of much of society.

For this reason, watching the new patterns of youth concern develop is a vital part of managing the human climate.

Despite the rapid changeability of youth, it is dangerous to ignore new youth movements as passing fads. On the other hand, it is also dangerous to take each one of them to be a sure sign of new directions and upheaval.

chapter 19 The urge for individuality and creativity

Mᴏʀᴇ and more people are having their sense of individual worth raised and their desire for self-expression honed by education, affluence, and free time.

After being exposed in college to the vast sunburst of variety that the world offers, few young people can ever return to parochial concentration on their original tight island of life.

Education opens the mind not like a cork removed from a bottle but like the entire lid removed from the top of a can—everything is exposed at the same time and the cover can never be plugged back in.

At the same time, the mechanization of most jobs and the growing domination of large organizations have been squeezing out the opportunity to be creative on the job and failing to provide a ready means toward individuality.

The individual may actually have a broader scope for his imagination and talents than the great majority of people in his grandfather's time, but the scope he finds available to him is far narrower than what he has been led to understand exists.

This anomaly is causing eruptions of individuality and self-expression in unlikely forms and places. The work scene has ceased to be where the action is for the stimulated youth of today.

Hair styles—facial and cranial—express revolt against conformity.

Sexual styles take new forms. With the concurrent assistance of the pill and the illusion that antibiotics make everything all right, individuality and creativity have taken over until the horizons of sex are limited more by dexterity and stamina than by underlying human relationships.

Marijuana and other mind-bending drugs probe inner sensitivities.

Playing a musical instrument; literally dabbling in art, needlepoint, and macramé; film-making; and other art forms attract millions of people with an urge for self-expression.

Hundreds of causes have found disciples who feel that by creating change they fulfill their urge to be creative.

Yet as each form of independent outlet gains followers, it loses its distinctiveness in the crowd. A form of creativity that attracts the individual seeking self-expression smothers individuality when it ceases to be distinctive and frustrates those who are early devotees.

The range of creative outlets is being used up rapidly. As the safety valve of such outlets in private lives fails to meet people's urges, there is likely to be a massive focusing of pressures on their job situations. Business and other employers are sure to be confronted with mounting demands for more meaningful jobs, job enrichment programs, a say for each employee on how the work is done and even on the purpose and nature of the organization itself.

Here is another factor of the human climate that is certain to command the attention of the managers of all our institutions.

chapter 20 The war of the two electronic revolutions

A significant struggle that will have important influence on the course of human events involves two nonhuman movements.

There are two electronic revolutions going on at the same time. They are both extremely powerful, and they are in direct conflict with each other.

One is the electronic revolution of television. It creates instant emotion and involvement in its audience. Each individual can feel himself engrossed in a dozen different spheres each day, often involving his emotions with more causes and events than his ancestors could feel in a lifetime.

Television puts strong emphasis on human feelings resulting from vicarious participation and the sense of being a spectator to human drama. Its format and appeal stress the rounding out of each problem with a neat and quick solution.

As a result, the effect of television is to emotionalize and personalize the response to events and to create impatience with slow-moving mechanisms and institutions.

As Marshall McLuhan pointed out in some of his emanations in *Understanding Media*, the electronic media have not only added to the means of communication; they have considerably transformed the outlook on life and the habits of thought of a large share of the human race.

In *The Information Machines*, Ben Bagdikian says: ". . . the swiftness and pervasiveness of modern communications . . . encourage reaction to minor, immediate events rather than major trends."

For a manager concerned with major trends and not day-to-day minutiae, this is a significant fact. It is compounded by the further fact cited by Bagdikian, which focuses on the problem of sensing what the public feels about events or issues: ". . . the present mass-communications system . . . is extraordinarily effective at carrying messages outward to the population, but it is almost useless in transmitting messages in the opposite direction."

Electronic media have partly displaced the slower, step-by-step communications process that involved considerable interchange between sender and receiver. This deprives managers of a vital means of sensing what people are thinking. It is a major factor in the growing segmentation and insulation of various elements of the population.

The computer revolution

The other electronic revolution involves the management of information and systems, exemplified by the computer. It stresses facts, organization, hard reality, and the elimination of nuisance variables.

As we have seen, the sophistication of our society that is necessary to approach meeting the expectations of the people depends on a massive organization of facts and processes that is possible only through computerization and automated mechanical processes. It is only through the extended use of computers and automation that it is possible to organize and operate the burgeoning systems needed to meet people's requirements and expectations—requirements and expectations that, to a large extent, have been built up by the multidimensional involvement of people by television.

Our youth are creatures of the TV revolution. This accounts for their strong sense of immediacy, human relationships, and the demand for ready answers to all problems. They insist that human considerations must overrule systems and organizations. They concentrate on the medium that provides no contact with the source. Because they see systems and organizations as being antithetical to their TV-generated sensitivities, they suspect them of being more inhumane and insensitive than they are.

Our system is based on rules, like computers. Television is based on emotion. Society is based on history and tradition. TV is based on immediacy and novelty.

There are scarcely any elements in America that have been progressing as rapidly as these two electronic forces. The impact of both these revolutions is massive. They appear to be on a collision course.

Managers are faced on one hand with increasing their ability to manage more complex operations, and on the other hand with accommodating to the growing Luddite antagonism to computerization.

Assessing these trends and finding a means of accommodating them is one of the greatest challenges facing the managers in our society.

chapter 21 An age of visibility and action

THE entire process by which human attitudes are established has been transformed by television, film, graphic publication, and the dramatic event.

It required the many millennia of human history to reach the point where a majority of people were partially literate. Now in less than a generation there has been an explosion of the graphic sense by which people obtain their impressions and their "knowledge."

Just as many primitive societies have been able to leapfrog years of industrial development by installing immediately the latest technologies, so many populations are bypassing the laborious process of becoming truly literate and finding in the visible media their source of information.

Marshall McLuhan sensed that a drastic change was occurring, but his diagnosis has proved faulty. The electronic and graphic media are not replacing the printed word but are adding major new dimensions to the information process. It is no longer possible to confine communications efforts to words, any more than we can confine transportation to the private carriage, however it may be propelled.

There is a multidimensional complex of communications to deal with, just as most other aspects of modern life have become multidimensional.

For managers, the vital fact is that visibility has instant impact. Both the instantaneous nature of visibility and the potency of its impact are crucial.

The nature of the change can be seen in the hero-making process.

Heroes used to be the creation primarily of historians and myth makers, carried out over a period of time. The imagination of the people was an important ingredient in processing a mortal man into a mythological hero. Now the process has been so speeded up and so changed that we have few heroes, and those that do emerge—such as Neil Armstrong, Martin Luther King, and John Wayne—are created by events as *seen* by the public through the creativity of the electronic myth makers. And the process that is speeded by electronics also hastens the shattering of the hero image. In days past, a person could remain a hero into history despite his limitations and frailties; but now figures made bigger than life with the aid of the TV tube—such as Edmund Muskie and George McGovern—crash to public mediocrity when the tube gives their real traits intensive exposure.

The reality of appearances

With immediacy and visual impact so predominant in the process that forms attitudes, thought in leisurely contemplation is at a great disadvantage against the visible and the active. The day when people reflected on what they heard and read was the day of the essay, the epic poem, and the great public address. Today we are in an era of this evening's news program and documentary, the motion picture, the demonstration, and orchestrated riots.

In this situation, what things *seem* to people to be is often the real reality, for it is what people base decisions on.

a. A carefully disciplined march or sit-in carried out by a minute fraction of a public came to mean a revolt by that entire public.

b. A few *avant garde* movies glorifying a counterculture that despised responsibility and discipline came to symbolize the supposed unanimity of an entire generation.

c. A few bra burnings and protest marches, fed upon by the "now" media, convinced millions that huge segments of the American female population were in revolt.

As a result, as we have seen, often the person or organization that feels a sense of responsibility and the need to base its actions on reason is at a disadvantage against the person or organization that has nothing to lose and can create the illusion of reality by irresponsible means.

Television, especially, misread its own potency and let itself be manipulated into an illusory device. When the reaction set in and responsible segments of the population responded in alarm, at first television felt it was the object of a plot of repression. Now it seems to be maturing in a realization of the revolution it has itself created in the communications process.

For the manager, the great significance of the emergence of this age of visibility and action is that settling for the previous processes of communicating is to settle for impotence.

New ideas and methods in managing the human climate are essential to survival. The revolution that has occurred in communications is as much a reality that management must assimilate as is the revolution in data processing and automation.

chapter 22 Segmentation of the populace

In a number of ways at the same time, the cohesion of the American public is being sundered.

In retrospect, it was one of the wonders of recent history that America—made up of many different peoples—formed a nation in which differences were more readily ironed out, and unified cooperation more readily achieved, than almost anywhere else on earth.

For nearly 100 years, following the Civil War, there were great sectional, ethnic, economic, and other differences, but we managed to attain a general unity of purpose. At the time, it seemed that there were chasms of difference between North and South, management and labor, rural and metropolitan; but from today's viewpoint we can recognize that most people had basically the same goals and were willing to give and take to get on with a national purpose.

Now the population is segmented in many ways.

It is almost evenly divided between those who have been trained primarily through written media and those who are visually oriented. The difference between these segments is far more than just what kind of communication reaches people. It is a fundamental difference in their entire outlook on life and the world.

Segmentation is also a consequence of the growing specialization in most fields of endeavor. Almost everyone is becoming more involved in the complexities of his field of interest. Each field tends to become more fragmented, with each individual concentrating his training and attention on a narrower segment. Accordingly, he devotes less attention to other fields or even segments of the broad field he is in, such as medicine, or law, or architecture; and at the same time, each field becomes less understandable to the others.

In spite of increased levels of education—which used to be considered the hope for broader understanding—education is intensifying specialization and therefore segmentation and alienation.

Forces for individual influence

A number of factors contribute to a strong movement toward every individual demanding a voice in every aspect of American life:

a. Mass education, as we have seen, magnifies the individual's sense of his worth and whets his appetite for participation.

b. Great increases in affluence provide the means and the time for individuals to involve themselves.

c. The visibility given to dissent by the media has acted as a lure to many to assert their dissatisfactions and demand "reforms."

d. Segmentation of our society has resulted in more people feeling alienated from a larger proportion of the total populace.

The expression by every individual of his preferences is the essence of democracy and individual freedom, but one of its effects finds the ignorant demanding control over education—as in ghetto parents' organizations insisting that they make the decisions for "their" schools.

Similarly, those who do not want to function in complex organizations—such as faculty members who have optioned out of the organizational "rat race"—insist that they must have a veto over how the organizations that employ them are run.

One of the most important aspects of the segmentation process is the women's rights movement. All the complaints being expressed by the spokeswomen for women's organizations have existed for millenia and have been substantially alleviated. The very release from household drudgery, frequent childbearing, and the constant perils of hunger and disease has freed American women to develop a new outlook. They have the time and the affluence to assert dissatisfaction and create perhaps the most critical of all the dissent movements.

People are scattering into various lifestyles.

Despite the mass of instantaneous communications that was supposed to iron out the differences between people, there is now as much variation between the hippie communes and the God-fearing, family-centered middle class as there was between Daniel Boone and the Brahmins of Emerson's Boston. In between, there is an array of outlooks on how life should be lived as varied as the more than 6750 listed magazines now published in the United States.

Political splintering

Segmentation is splintering the traditional political processes. Continuation of the two-party system is a fiction that is perpetuated by accidents and happenstance rather than similarity of viewpoints. The Roosevelt coalition of big-city workers, blacks, other ethnic groups, and intellectuals no longer coalesces into a Democratic party. Richard Nixon was re-elected more by a coalition of elements unable to accept George McGovern than by any identification with Republicanism.

And fractionalization of the family is eroding the structure that used to give almost everyone at least one basic meeting ground. With Father and Mother both working, many homes resemble more a subway station where people regularly pass through than a cohesive unity.

The nonexistence of the nuclear family in fact, in many instances, is being recognized in the many substitute forms of social combination that are being propounded. Multiple marriage, open marriage, nonmarriage, *menage à trois ou quatre*, gay liaisons, and a wide variety of other liaisons all have their enthusiasts. More and more, when youngsters get together the question is no longer, "Who are your mommy and daddy?" but "Where?"

It might be said that at least the publics of concern to a manager have in common their humanness; but then the question arises, what are the traits of today's human? The variety of orientations is vast and seems to be growing constantly.

It used to be said that "you can't change human nature"; now we not only find human nature changing in multiple ways, we also face the difficulty of determining whether there are *any* traits that are really basic to human nature.

chapter 23   The mass production of mediocrity

NOT only is the lovingly handcrafted product disappearing before the pressures of mass production; the opportunity and recognition for the uniquely capable person is being drowned in the tidal wave of attention to the inept and the stupid.

Here again, the contradictions of the intelligentia stumble over each other. On one hand there is the insistence that all persons are unique beings and that the great dilemma of the individual is to determine who he is and where his uniqueness lies. To most people in the Western world, who have had the shackles of struggle for mere existence broken, the fulfillment of the self is their reason for being.

Alarm about central information banks, the depersonalization of huge corporations, the homogeneity of the armed forces, the IBM file of the multiversity, the surveillance of police . . . all these alarms are based on fear of oppression by an affluent society, which has replaced the oppressions of want and theology as the terror of man.

This concern is based on our awareness that there is an almost infinite range of possible genetic variations in the human species.

The more we learn about the DNA molecule, the more we are aware of the vast range of differences that exist among beings. While each of us results from an unbroken line of genetic heritages stretching back to the first stirring of one-cell life, each of us comes into the world with his own never-repeated encoding of traits and cells.

A regiment of intellectual seers points to the reluctance of young people to participate in what has been called the "megamachine" as evidence that they cherish this sense of individuality above all else. The canons of law put the uniqueness of the individual above the needs of society: no general decrees can be applied; each person is entitled to his own day in court and the full range of appeals. Medicine is chastised for tendencies to overlook the need of each person for individual treatment and attention.

Yet the very intelligentsia whose new religion is the uniqueness of the person, insist there must be sameness—what they call equality—in all the earth's 3,500,000,000 persons.

Our entire economy is twisted to seek the goal of equal distribution of benefits to all regardless of individual contribution or merit. The political structure is distorted to give equal voice to those who are illiterate and unwise. Education sets its goal at uplifting the stupid to savants. The living and social patterns of all segments of society are attacked to make way for forced inclusion of the inept, on the basis that their mere existence entitles them to equal sharing in the fruits of achievement.

Sydney J. Harris, who prides himself on his liberalism, points out that in the half-dozen years up to mid-1972, more than $500,000,000 were spent to improve the education of "disadvantaged" children; and during that time, the number of underachieving pupils increased.

Reversed priorities

In the avalanches of debate over forced integration of schools, the overwhelming justification has been the need to uplift the lower segment of the student population. Greater and greater proportions of the resources in countless school systems have been shifted to this elusive end.

When cuts must be made because of competing demands, it is the specialized programs for the nonordinary student that usually must be abandoned. Schools are penalized for giving attention to the talented person who could have great contributions to make and are forced to pull standards down to keep submarginal students afloat. This continues in the face of findings such as those of the team headed by Christopher Jencks of Harvard, as reported in the *New York Times*, that as long as people assume that economic quality for the poor can be achieved by "ingenious manipulations of marginal institutions like the schools, progress will remain glacial."

The pressures on colleges to employ quotas of minority members and women have at last evoked protests from educators who feel, on the basis of what they view the purpose of the institution to be, that merit should be the primary basis for employment.

In the name of equal opportunity, opportunity is thus denied to the gifted to fulfill themselves, and their gifts are denied to a society that calls this homogenization "progress."

This process is being carried into postschool years. Employers are increasingly being forbidden to test the intelligence and trainability of their potential employees. The City Commission on Human Rights of New York City has even forbidden employers to check on the arrest and conviction records of applicants.

The United States combined the ethic of hard work and individual gain, the great power of universal opportunity, and a wealth of resources to become predominant during the century between 1860 and 1960. But the delusions we have bred out of that experience are now on the verge of sending us the way of the Greeks, the Romans, the early Chinese, and the British.

The London form of the virus was marked by the syndrome of "I'm all right, Jack." The New York variety is epitomized in "I've got it made."

The international challenge

The competition between peoples and nations provides the thrust to keep the human system evolving. Though we show throughout our society the symptom of taking what we have for granted and agitating for more, whether we get more or even hold what we have will be determined not by our demands but by how we meet the conditions of the 1970s and 1980s in competition with peoples who know they have yet to make it.

Our corporation executives may prefer the comfort of long weekends and football on color TV to making sales in Africa and India, but the Russians and Chinese do not.

Our union members have made a monopoly and use it to force higher and higher labor costs, while workers in Hong Kong and Singapore and Tokyo still emphasize the need to produce.

Millions of our youth consider employment in productive work either crass or exploitative, but Spaniards and Italians still flock to West Germany for the chance to get jobs where they can work hard.

American university faculties disdain the function of preparing young people to fill useful roles in a productive society. They direct their best students into fields aimed at manipulation—government, social work, and proliferation of those who have trouble coping with our complex society.

Russia, China, Japan, and Germany unabashedly seek more

managers, engineers, practicing doctors, and instructors of practical subjects. American pundits create expectations for the 30-hour week and predict we will soon need no one to do physical work.

There has been a widespread effort to tell Americans they can unilaterally drop out of the competitive world and still continue having more and working less. This climate has been developed, ironically, by the same intellectual cadre who a few years ago were the loudest in proclaiming we could not isolate ourselves from the rest of the world.

All the world is explosively striving to come close to our living standards. The resources in demand—oil, copper, nickel, manganese; air and pure water—become more and more inadequate. Our dependence on our ability to compete becomes ever more acute. Our ability to sell our exports goes down. More and more, we are coming to believe that we are beyond the need for discipline, that we can afford the luxury of letting any individual choose his own form of goofing off.

Managers, almost by definition, are achievement oriented. They must have goals and measure their effectiveness in terms of what they accomplish. The mass production of mediocrity—enforced by government power—is a direct denial of the concept of achievement.

This aspect of today's human climate in America is another of the challenges to management that mark the new front line of critical decision making.

SECTION III The organizations

chapter 24 The crucial importance of communication

AMERICAN managers like to think they are the spearheads in the advance of change. They lament the fact that often their efforts to bring about change are slowed by the inertia of our institutions and traditions. It has become a truism, albeit unexamined, that businessmen are the real radicals in our society because they are constantly pressing forward the limits of innovation, while other elements in our society are slow in keeping pace.

Yet many managers continue to function as though the relationships between various groups are different only in degree from what they were a generation ago. They see these groups as entities they must cope with—as the objects of their efforts to overcome resistance to new products or services, new corporate forms, new routes to efficient uses of manpower, and so on.

The misjudgment of the extent to which the dynamics of our society have changed can be seen in the attitude of many managers toward communication.

Perhaps no aspect of management has received as much attention or inspired so many books as the broad subject of communication. A bibliography of the important books and articles on the subject in recent years would itself produce a substantial book.

Besides the treatments that deal directly with communication, the essence of many other subjects is really communication, from much of what is written about marketing to the basic philosophies of management; from the X and Y theory of Douglas McGregor to the *Managerial Psychology* of Harold Leavitt.

The innovations and fads that sweep managerial enthusiasms periodically, including group dynamics and transactional analysis, are really gropings for greater expertness in communication.

The common concept of the role of communication in management might be summed up by the statement of Harold Leavitt that the concern of managers about communication is appropriate "because communication is indeed a critical dimension of organization."

A perceptive analysis of all of this concern about communication among managers, however, reveals one predominant fact. Overwhelmingly, it treats communication as a *tool* of management. It is seen as something the manager needs to know how to use just as he needs to know something of business law, accounting, distribution, and marketing.

This may well be the reason that so much of management's communication is ineffective and, indeed, often backfires with effects opposite to those desired.

The nine roles of communication

Communication is no longer a tool of management, an instrument for conveying decisions. Communication is the *substance* of decision. Communication determines what any function or decision of any organization really turns out to be, because it determines what will happen.

In essence, there are five ways that most managers visualize the role of communication:

1. *To report.* When actions are taken, policies established, plans developed, communication is seen as the next step to convey that information to the audiences involved.

2. *To instruct.* Management says: "Following the recommendations of our systems analyst, from now on we will use this procedure in handling requests for the working files on policyholders. . . ."

3. *To order.* Management says: "To remain within the budget available for guard service on the parking lot, employees are notified that they must have their cars removed by 5:30 P.M."

4. *To persuade.* Management says: "The company's latest proposal to the bargaining committee of the Union represents an exceptionally generous advancement in compensation and benefits, and we urge that the membership let its leaders know that they accept it."

5. *To inoculate.* Communication is devoted to reporting on the good works of the company and its dedication to corporate responsibility, as an investment in forestalling criticism on these and other matters.

Many enlightened managers also see two other roles for communication:

6. Acknowledging that true communication is two-way, they are alert to the inputs received from the audiences and consider them in devising policies and developing statements.

7. As the lubricant of relations between people, communication is recognized as a necessity in working out differences between management and other groups such as government agencies, labor organizations, local communities, and minority groups.

But there are still two other dimensions that are vital yet rarely recognized:

8. Achieving a harmony of purpose, understanding, and pace among the many elements involved in the operation of the organization. Any organization may be compared with an orchestra, in which the different elements may be playing different scores and yet together they must produce a unified harmony. In the coordination of diverse elements of the organization, communication should be the metronome that sets the beat.

9. Properly planned and executed communications can create the *same* conception of any situation in the minds of all, as nearly as possible. We have seen that what something seems to be becomes the reality in the minds of the beholders. It is increasingly vital to use communication effectively to make certain that what things seem to be and the reality are the same for all the publics involved.

It is possible for each segment of an organization to perform its defined functions perfectly and yet for the entire organization to be beset with problems and inefficiencies. It is the potential of truly effective communication to knit together the understanding and cohesion necessary to produce a pleasingly orchestrated effect.

chapter 25   Numbers that lie

I is commonplace for managers to castigate the seemingly unstoppable tendency of government bureaucracy to build the numbers of employees.

The remarkable success of Parkinson's Law when it was propounded a few years ago can be attributed to the instantaneous recognition of its validity: "Work expands so as to fill the time available for its completion."

It is one of the primary traits of the good manager to be on the alert for an accumulation of bodies in various offices out of proportion to the functions performed. The sophisticated techniques of work measurement, incentives, and other devices have been developed to forestall this common failing. Particularly since the blood-letting recession of 1970, more and more managements seek to have permanent mechanisms for measuring the functions performed in terms of the people involved.

In many fields a relationship can be established between the size of the staff and the results. This is true, for instance, in such activities as billing, the production line, typing, filing, and even sales.

However, the constant temptation to evaluate management of human-climate areas in terms of manpower and payroll encounters entirely different criteria.

Managements that are accustomed to checking their efficiency ratios in any field against industry norms or tabulations published by an outside research organization often try to do the same in public relations, public affairs, and other people-dependent functions. But the principal factor in all human-climate areas is the quality of mind brought to the challenge. Planning manpower and budgets in terms of numbers is no more effective than commissioning a great play or a musical masterpiece by the entire faculty of a conservatory just because their talents are presumed to add up to more than those of any one member.

A few creative, qualified, and dedicated people are usually the moving factor in every successful effort to sway people—not the number of bodies or the size of the budget.

It is a safe rule that any effort to plan or evaluate a program in this area in terms of numbers—whether people, pieces of paper produced, dollars, or any other criterion—is likely to be wrong.

There are, for instance, many cases of industry programs aimed at changing the habits of the American people that spent $500,-000 a year and more, year after year, with little demonstrable result, while one group, with a budget that averaged well under $100,000 a year, achieved one of the most memorable successes of any industry program. That was the American Music Conference, representing the various elements of the musical merchandise industry, during the years 1948 through 1967.

Applying numbers as the guide to evaluation in human-climate areas is not only likely to be unneccessarily expensive. It is also likely to predetermine failure of the effort, because it emphasizes the machinery and the motions rather than the ideas and the emotions.

It is what happens in the minds of the audience that counts, not what happens in the offices of the organization.

chapter 26 Getting lost in a shell

MOST organizations continue to focus on their established ways of functioning while the conditions affecting them are being revolutionized.

Business devotes most of its attention to production, finance, and marketing—while its existence is being challenged on the issues of consumerism, minority hiring, preservation of the environment, invasion of management functions by labor and government, the reluctance of bright young people to work in large companies, and other forces that are all in the minds of men.

Doctors continue to focus on caring for patients and their fees—while vocal groups clamor for restructuring the health care system, drafting doctors for areas that lack them, and other issues that are in the minds of men.

The colleges, despite their traumatic tumult of recent years, are still essentially concerned with courses, budgets, faculty, and research—while vocal groups and government assault them to revolutionize not only their structures and functions but their very reasons for being.

All these fields and others labor conscientiously in their vineyards. But the climate of attitudes that will determine whether they will be able to function at all—and on whose terms—is being developed by the outside forces that shape public attitudes.

It is characteristic of the expansion of our expectations that almost no one can any longer count on the conscientious fulfillment of his function to maintain his security. The builder of a better mousetrap in the 1970s and 1980s not only will find that no path is beaten to his door, but his tenure as an entrepreneur will be a short one unless he is able to manage the host of human-climate requirements: attracting and dealing with a work force, probably including one or more unions; avoiding the suspicion of ecologists that his supply of wood rapes the land and that his waste products foul the atmosphere; dealing with the local license bureau and zoning board; and many others.

For the manager, this is part of the growing need to resist imposing structuralization and measurability on every aspect of his function. He must take a broad, diverse, and flexible approach —especially in including human-climate factors in all his considerations.

Charles E. Summer, Jr., of the Graduate School of Business at Columbia University says:

. . . when he is making decisions as a member of top management, [the executive] must vigorously resist the temptation to become beholden to any one point of view. This is a problem which is generally insignificant for scientists, lawyers, doctors, and so on. By contrast, the heterogeneity of [an] organization requires a very high order of judgment and mental discipline on the part of the manager.

A common point of view among managers is a stress on tangibility and "tough mindedness." They also need mental discipline to cover the ephemeral but vital forces in human attitudes.

chapter 27 The illusion of perfectability

THE sense that anything is attainable underlies the classic American optimism.

Written in the minds of many people is the slogan that only in America could be taken seriously: "The difficult we do immediately; the impossible takes longer."

It is presumed that once we find the right organization, the right motivations, the right ways to overcome the doubters and the foot-draggers, perfection will be achieved.

As a result, much of the activity of every organization is a quest worthy of a Don Quixote, a search for the perfect operation. What perfection would be is not defined. No two people would describe it the same way. But there is tacit agreement that when things really get organized, perfection will be attained.

Yet even if the ultimate miracle should be achieved and a condition that all agreed was perfection should be reached, that would require a state of arrest—the end of all change—because any change from perfection would mean to lose perfection. Since one of the few certainties is that change is constant, perfection could not last more than a moment.

The illusion of perfectability is a Holy Grail with some justification as a motivation for managers and their staffs, even though it can never be attained. But it is also an increasing challenge to every organization as it becomes a motivating force among many of the publics it must deal with.

a. Consumerists are uncompromising in setting their goal as zero defects.
b. Conservationists consider acceptable conditions for extraction of raw materials to be zero effect on the environment.
c. Those concerned with pollution set zero emission as an unflagging goal.
d. There are articulate advocates for zero unemployment, zero health problems, and so on.

The American illusion of perfectability—that anything short of absolute goals is a sign of treachery and sabotage—is another of the pressing human-climate challenges that faces the management of all our institutions.

chapter 28   Is there nothing in a name?

As we have seen, visibility is a growing need for all organizations. The importance of establishing a clear and distinctive identity for each organization has moved many managements to undertake substantial advertising, public relations, and public affairs programs. At the same time, the growing complexity and diversification of many companies is making it more difficult for the public to visualize the character of the organization as a whole.

An individual has a distinctive face, his own fingerprints, mannerisms that are his alone that help differentiate him from all other persons. But an organization—even to its employees or members—does not have a visible front or delineated characteristics. Accordingly, its name is even more important in establishing its identity than is the name for a person.

Names—usually originated with the confident assurance that they will stamp the organization with a distinctive identity for all time—have been among the most affected aspects of organizations' adjustment to our period of rapid changes. Companies find their original products or services have become obsolete and have been replaced by entirely different ones. Companies that began to serve a given location become national and international. Companies that were dedicated to intensive specialization become diversified or even conglomerate.

As a result, in recent years there has been a wholesale process of name changing, aimed at shedding names that have become outdated, misidentifying, or limiting. At the same time, it has become popular to simplify company names following the theory that the public is more likely to remember a short name than a long one.

But now we find that efforts to "simplify" company names have bred confusion and blurred images, rather than clarified identities and sharpened images.

Seeking names that are not misnomers, some companies have adopted names that are not names at all.

On the New York Stock Exchange alone there are more than 100 companies with names that are initials or coined esoteric syllables. Many are recognized only by their employees and a few others. After years of trying, only a few companies with initial names have achieved wide identity—such as RCA, IBM and A. & P. Uniroyal is a rare case of establishing recognition for a coined name.

Under the letter "A" alone in the New York Stock Exchange daily listings appear the following:

ACF	AMP
AJ	APL
AMBAC	ARA
AMF	

Under "A" in the New York Stock Exchange listings appear these coined names:

AIRCO	AMFAC
AKZONA	AMPEX
ALCO Standard	AMREP

AMSTAR	ARCATA
AMSTED	ARMCO
AMTEL	ARO
ANCORP	ATO
APCO	AVCO
APECO	

In 1972 alone, these name changes were effected—most of them moving from distinctive and recognizable names to hard-to-remember compounds:

New Name	*Old Name*
CL Financial	Vanguard International
CLC of America	Consolidated Leasing Corporation of America
Codesco Inc.	Consolidated Dental Services
Conrock Company	Consolidated Rock Products
HMW Industries	Hamilton Watch Co.
INTEXT, Inc.	International Textbook
LTV Corp.	Ling-Temco-Vought
MLS Industries	Monterey Life Systems
MoAmCo	Mobile Americana
PACCAR, Inc.	Pacific Car & Foundry
Pasco, Inc.	Pan American Sulphur
PVO International	Pacific Vegetable Oil
RAI Inc.	Ramer Industries
TCC Inc.	Tracor Computing Corp.
UV Industries	U.S. Smelting, Refining and Mining
WHDH Corp.	Boston Herald Traveler

It may be granted that many companies find they have outgrown their names for various reasons—getting out of the industry mentioned, bad publicity of a previous management, and others. But the drastic lack of recognition resulting from such a naming process at least indicates a lack of sensitivity to how people form their attitudes.

One of the basic principles of names is that the right degree of distinctiveness—not too difficult, but not commonplace or meaningless—is important if the owner of the name is to make a lasting impression.[1]

It is easier to remember Martin Morrison than it is 384–1093. Henry Josephson is remembered more easily than John Johnson. It is easier to distinguish between Annotated Notes Company and Amplified Notions Systems than it is between ANC and ANS.

The loss of identity that may result from this lack of recognition can be costly.

The name is the distillation of what the company is and stands for in people's minds. It is much more its "image" than any emblem or logotype, on which thousands of companies have spent large sums. The recognition it creates affects its impression among prospective employees, potential investors, dealers, customers, and others. Coupon returns from direct response advertisements decreased by 50 percent after Smith-Corona-Marchant changed its name to SCM Corp.[2]

Factors in choosing a name

While there are many approaches to the selection of a new name, each of which has its proponents, it is important that the basic elements involved in the choice of a name be kept in mind during considerations. These include:

1. It must be euphonious—pleasant to the ear, easy to say, not subject to such mispronunciation as is common with Ruberoid and Chemetron.

2. It must be memorable—avoiding names that are too commonplace, such as "Smith," "National," "Universal," etc.; and easy to remember.

3. It should create a feeling of friendliness and warmth, if possible; a good name of a person would be preferable to an institutional name like "Standard" or "Empire." The word "Corporation" is likely to create more resistance than "Company."

4. It should be timeless. It must not only be effective and suitable for the present, but safe from any conceivable developments of the future. It should not be associated with any techniques, kind of product, or other factor that could be out-dated or limited by future events.

It is possible, for instance, that companies now using the name "National" will soon be embarrassed in their efforts to exploit worldwide markets; and, going further into the future, should these companies adopt "International" they may have to change later to "Interplanetary."

5. The name should be all-inclusive, so it in no way limits future possibilities. For example, Hotpoint was a good name for an electric iron but somewhat anomalous on a refrigerator; Frigidaire is good for a refrigerator but not on a range. At the speed with which business and industry are developing, it is hardly possible now to predict what any company may be identified with 30 years in the future.

6. It must be unduplicated—not only in its own business but, if possible, in any area of business. This is not only important in preventing confusion and legal complications; it can be devastating if a company in any line, having a similar name, should run into very unfavorable publicity.

7. Similarly, the name must have good associations in the minds of all groups of people. It should not bring up unpleasant connotations or prejudices. As nearly as possible it should be a good "neutral" name.

8. It should be conducive to use in a logotype, on labels, and in other printed forms. Some combinations of letters are hard to

distinguish at a glance or a distance, such as COATES, where the capital "C" and capital "O" look so much alike.

9. It should be registerable in all countries.

10. It should have quick acceptability—not requiring a slow memorization or recognition process.

chapter 29 Creating one's own competition

ANOTHER symptom of the failure of many managers to recognize the dynamics of the changing human climate is the simultaneous pursuit of opposite goals.

At the same time they recognize that change is the dominant factor affecting an organization's planning, they devote much of their attention to solidifying their positions, products, and markets as if they could be shielded from change.

The effort of organizations to protect their positions and to freeze a good setup leaves in the hands of outsiders the initiative for the modifications that are sure to come. And in many cases, it actually encourages new competition.

A good example is the television broadcasting industry. In trying to hold onto a very good thing, it has opened the way for expensive and long-germinating competition that would otherwise be a less-attractive venture: public television, cable television, videotape players for the home. It has given the movie, newspaper and magazine industries as a whole a long time to adjust and stay prosperous while they compete with television.

The television industry found the formula for large and comfortable profits through a homogenized offering of programming, with little difference among the various networks and the independent producers. While the population was segmenting into many different interest groups and tastes were spreading in many directions, this concentration on the vast middle ground of programming left untapped large segments of the total spectrum of potential program offerings. Entrepreneurs, instead of being discouraged by the large investments, regulatory hurdles, long development periods, and competitive uncertainties, found the possibilities attractive enough to clamor for entry.

Similarly, the efforts of the radio broadcasting industry to forestall reasonable limits on radio commercials have been the reason makers of tape players in cars and stereo units for the home—despite their initially high prices—have done so well. Millions of people now gladly pay to avoid having to listen to the air pollution of most radio broadcasting.

Other examples abound.

• The manufacturers of standard typewriters bypassed new-product development and allowed IBM to capture the bulk of the lucrative market with its electrics.

• The large, established food producers were not the ones who developed the fast-freezing process; it was the lone researcher Clarence Birdseye.

• The American automobile manufacturers were so pleased with their tight control of the auto market in the United States until about 1950 that they felt they were the determiners of what kind of automobile the American people would buy. When Volkswagen and Renault first demonstrated that the American producers were creating an opening for competitors, the Detroit producers first ridiculed the possibility that Americans would buy such small units in quantity, and then rushed out their own compacts to compete. The lesson was a brief one, however, because the compacts soon became larger and costlier and

Toyota, Datsun, and Mazda joined the group of importers who welcomed this opening.

• It was not until *The Saturday Evening Post* and *Look* met their demise that Time, Inc., recognized that the era of the general mass-circulation magazine had passed and the specialized publication was taking over. By failing to use its vast resources, experience, and staffs to move early into the specialized-interest areas, Time, Inc., watched *Life* fade away while *Psychology Today*, *Playboy*, *Cosmopolitan*, and other special-interest publications prospered.

America is a society that has always relished change and abhorred stagnation. In the multiple dynamics of our present shifting culture, a locked-in position is not a bulwark but an immobile target.

The pattern for winning the competitive battles of today and tomorrow is not the Maginot line but the fluid mobility of a force always probing for the initiative in bringing about its own changes.

SECTION IV Other dynamics of the people factor

chapter 30 The trap of formulas

T̲ʜᴇ masterful manager of the seventies has been trained to demand facts and proof. He tends to be uneasy with immeasurable factors and plans that have no precedent behind them. The ideal manager is said to expect his staff to "come to me with answers."

Business and other organizations have been moving strongly toward using computers and other quantifying and predicting techniques to "get answers" and to "organize efficiently."

The leading concept in graduate schools of business relates all studies and considerations to the case-study method. While there is room for imagination and innovation, the student is trained to put together building blocks of tangible facts and logic that add up to a visible "solution" for each case.

In his training years, the young manager is weighed in terms of the specific responses he makes to specific problems or assignments. He is evaluated periodically, often with a numerical scale. Measurements that go into his dossier are based on the predictions and expectations at the beginning of a period and the measurable consequences at the close of it.

This discipline works excellently wherever there are measurable and predictable factors.

- The manager can judge the likelihood of success in most matters of the law because the law is based on precedents, codified previous cases, and the recorded actions taken on similar matters by the courts.

- In architecture and plant design, there are blueprints and diagrams down to the smallest detail.

- In purchasing, almost every product is bought on the basis of detailed specifications.

- In accounting, the statements and ledgers are mathematical purity itself, with every number in its precise position in an orderly tabulation.

- Finance moves to the discipline of numbers and values that, despite monetary fluctuations, fit the specific pattern that the disciplined manager expects.

- Production can increasingly be spelled out in specifics, with the aid of the computer, from specification of raw materials through location of sources and transportation all along the chain of the production process.

So it goes with virtually all the areas that today's manager has been trained to deal with.

The elusiveness of attitudes

However, when this technique is applied to the people factor, or the human climate, it tends to create problems rather than solve them.

Managing the human climate calls for dealing with *changes* in attitudes—sensing what they will be but have never been— rather than getting readings based on precedent, patterns, or formulas. It is necessary to lead the target, not follow it.

Human attitudes are notoriously ephemeral and changeable. Managements uneasy about this have pressed for means of getting tabulations of opinions and attitudes so they will have "the numbers" on a comparable basis with the other areas of their concern. But measurements of attitudes, except for special events such as elections, are uncertain and subject to wide error. Gallup or Louis Harris are able to predict rather precisely how voters will respond in a major election because the voters have a strong concern about such an election and think about it enough to form an opinion before the pollster reaches them. But when a question is asked about whether the price of aluminum is too high or whether there should be a smaller variety of packages on a supermarket shelf, the answers given are as ephemeral as predictions of next year's stock market levels.

Rather than being predictable, the vast majority of human attitudes are most likely to differ at other times and in other circumstances from what they have been. Deep-felt concerns such as religious belief, ethnic identity, self-worth, and a few others are stubbornly constant; those that touch the individual slightly tend to be as changeable as styles.

Accordingly, there is great danger in basing plans for coping with the human climate on what has gone before, either within the organization itself or in other situations that are supposedly comparable. In fact, the variables are so great and the ephemeral nature of attitudes is so important, plans and programs that worked somewhere else are most likely *not* to be sound for a different situation, a different time, or a different organization.

This is of vital importance for the manager because failure to recognize it can increase the likelihood of failure. Demanding plans that "add up" like a production schedule downgrades the emphasis that the planners will give to the essential creativity and originality.

Many practitioners in public relations and public affairs, in fact, take advantage of this propensity of management in selling their services. They develop a formula with as many specifics and hard promises as they can. They point to what has been done for another organization in other circumstances. They cite surveys of opinions taken at other times. It thus becomes easy to develop a "basic presentation" that, with the change of a few pages, is offered to a gamut of potential clients.

It is a safe rule that when any presentation follows such a formula approach, the manager should lock up his checkbook.

It is tempting for the public relations person to hold back any immeasurable, unpredictable, unprecedented recommendations if he knows that his management considers them to be "fuzzy thinking." Yet most of the time it is exactly the unprecedented and the immeasurable creativity that make possible real changes in group attitudes.

So there is always danger that the more effort that is made to apply standards of prediction and measurement to human-climate matters, the more emphasis will be placed on the superficial—and the more difficult it will be to make progress against the real problems.

Many managers have been disillusioned with the programs they have authorized that have failed to gain a better rapport with their publics, yet many of these failures in dealing with human attitudes are the result of managers insisting on being sure the plans "check out" in advance . . . that they follow an approved formula.

It is a safe rule that human attitudes and actions will always find ways to defy efforts to harness them to rigid patterns. The manager is wise to steer clear of formula approaches to the human climate.

chapter 31   Perils of the "tight ship"

ANOTHER concept of today's professional manager is that a business should be structured along lines of responsibility; and that each sector and, as much as possible, each person should be accountable for a specified objective.

The practice of structuring companies into profit centers follows this concept. If a group is given the responsibility for achieving specific profit goals, then its responsibilities must be defined and its functions spelled out in detail.

Services that are called on by various profit centers are asked to perform specific functions and to allocate their time and costs accordingly.

This is a discipline of management that becomes increasingly necessary as organizations become more complex and diversified.

However, managements that work by tough-minded application of manpower to targeted needs can prove to be the least flexible.

The defined allotment of functions and responsibilities makes for an orderly structure of human units within the operation and satisfies the manager's desire for being able to measure the work and results of each person.

Pigeonholing people to meet specifications precisely works in the short range. Profit goals set neat parameters for each operation. That in turn makes it easier to set targets for the following quarter or year. Work flows and outputs can be measured between comparable operations in various offices and between individuals with similar functions, so the tightening of personnel requirements and salary standards can be based on measurable tabulations.

However, this type of pigeonholing tends to make both the company and its people vulnerable to the changes that are inevitable. The structured operation based on guidelines, especially when they lean heavily on past measurements, solidifies a structure so that it may not be able to change its direction fast enough.

Thousands of trained people have found that the skills they had burnished in their special niches were obsolete when recession struck and they were out of jobs.

The pigeonholed structure is a movement toward limiting the range of the individual employee, at a time when the pressures are building among employees against limitation on the individual worker. The tight personnel structure becomes a tight collar for the employee in an office position or "junior management," just as tight job limitations in assembly plants build deadening monotony into the job.

Treating people as units

It is not a coincidence that the organization chart so basic to the "tight ship" concept of management closely resembles the layout diagram of a factory or office. Management seeks the comfort of assigning a precise place and role for each person, just as there is a precise place and function for each machine or bank of desks. And just as the equipment on a factory floor is considered subject to moving about and realignment, so the organization chart presumes that each individual may be moved from one pigeonhole to another without changing his scope or dimensions.

The "tight ship" stultifies the development and contribution of the great majority of employees, who are shown that anything outside their limited assignments is unwelcome from them. Thus a major percentage of the total *potential* creativity and intelligence of hundreds or thousands of people is foreclosed from benefiting the company. Such narrowing of each individual's creativity and input atrophies his potential, with resulting mass waste of human capacities and enthusiasm.

The ramifications go even further than the existing work force. The best young people—upon whom any organization's future depends—shun companies that stratify their personnel. They want to see that the company makes room for movement, variety, and broad participation. To them, a tightly structured organization is not symptomatic of good management but a lifetime sentence to frustration and boredom.

Much has been said recently about the virtues of participation management. Participation management means not only instilling varied input into operations and decisions; it calls for making the boxes on the organization chart elastic and maneuverable. The job definition of each person can be redefined to open up and encourage inputs and critiques on any aspect of the business—perhaps especially those aspects not involved in the job description.

This type of participation management assures more flexibility for the organization, and greater enthusiasm and fulfillment for the people. It is a means of making a career in an organization attractive to the educated and critical younger generation, and of alleviating the sinking regard the public holds for all the institutions in our society.

31   Perils of the "tight ship"

Tough-minded managers have long prided themselves on operating a tight ship. In today's human climate, the organization that
is too clearly a tight ship may be flying danger signals. It may be
too tight to meet the buffets of future change.

chapter 32 The systems approach to the human climate

THE experiences of the 1960s should carry a lesson of great importance to every manager. During that decade the United States showed two historic sides. One of them was the exploration of space. It was decided in 1960 that before the end of the decade we would land a man on the moon.

On the other side were the developments in the human-climate areas. Despite the great promises raised by Presidents Kennedy and Johnson about a new era and a Great Society, the conflicts and turmoils in human relations cascaded toward the brink of chaos and disaster. We bogged down in the labyrinth of Vietnam; we had riots in Watts and Detroit; we had takeovers of college campuses, bombings of public buildings, a spiraling increase in crime, and a general breakdown in relations among segments of the population.

The lesson here is that both the area of space exploration and the area of human relations were approached as if they were essentially the same. It was widely believed that if we set our minds on solving our human problems, if we appropriated enough money and assigned enough manpower, we could achieve whatever objective we set.

But the moon is a fixed target. Scientists could predict in 1960 exactly where it would be on July 20, 1969. No other circumstances would change the nature or the scope of the challenge.

The moon-landing program was a triumph of the "systems approach," which weighs all the interrelated factors together and tries out many "models" and "scenarios" to see not only what their outcome would be, but also what the unexpected side effects might be. All conceivable elements are fed into the considerations together; and the interplay between them is accounted for in the calculations, in planning, and in patient trial. All signals are "no go" until the systems mesh on a sound course.

The specific and visible task of exploring space imposes nonhuman frailties. It forces each expert to intermesh with all the alien specialists. If he does not, the computer shows the red light or the simulator spins out of orbit. The food chemist and the television monitor's monitor are bolted together with the astronomer and the geologist into a system of intellects that must match the system of technical entities.

The space program is a macrocosm of the ideal in the mind of the master manager. He seeks to zero in on a problem by isolating it so it can be studied in detail and attacked in peace. He wants to be able to get a reading on how various elements will react with each other and then to choose the best of many alternatives.

The differences in human problems

However, all the problems that revolve around human attitudes are much like the problems of social disillusion that menaced our society in the 1960s. They are not absolutes that retain exact identity for as long as we want to study them.

Their interrelationship with each other is not predictable like a chemical formula or a mechanical action. The problems are part of an interrelated complex of human vagaries and sensitivities. They affect each other and change each other constantly, so that none of them is quite the same at two different points in time. In affecting each other, they affect many facets of the organization. Coping with them calls for a systems approach far different from the systems approach of the space program, which permitted studying and coordinating isolated elements.

As in any system, the elements that go into coping with a network of interrelated human problems must be developed and carried out together. If any of them gets too much push, that in itself creates new stresses and the whole system is likely to go out of whack.

The interplay of many elements within a system—technological or human—is a vast system of checks and balances. The resistance of each element to losing its own equilibrium is matched against the pressure of other elements to alter that equilibrium. Each element changes and in turn changes others. Together they move along the limited spectrum of modification that is possible. When one element pushes too hard, somewhere in the interplay of forces a counterforce must arise to wrench it back into line.

Extreme attention, for instance, to productivity can have repercussions in employee relations, pollution problems, dealer relations, and other areas. All elements must be planned in balance and all must advance and develop in balance . . . with constant sensitivity to how that balance is being maintained.

The interdependence of all the elements of our society—and of any organization—is visible all about us. The impossibility of isolating any human function and having it operate effectively on its own is evident.

Francis Bacon said, more than 350 years ago: "It is a secret both in nature and State, that it is safer to change many things than one."

Our failure, three-and-a-half centuries later, to recognize this wisdom is another reflection of our overspecialization.

In his own field, every expert knows that there are no absolute "answers." The mark of the mature expert is his recognition of the limitations to his expertness, the need for qualifying his judgments. But in all other fields he is impatient that the "answers" are not forthcoming, that the specialists plead for weighing alternatives and making careful study and not upsetting the delicate balance.

In his own field, each man tends to be a conservative because he knows he doesn't know enough to make rapid changes. In viewing all other fields he is a liberal, eager to see changes he "knows" should be made.

Ministers castigate business and government for being "unresponsive"—but resist bitterly bringing the role of the church into confluence with a world view of the 1970s.

Educators who cherished their isolation from the crass competitive system trained generations of restless youth to attack the workings of that system—and cringe in impotence when the whirlwind of explosive young arrogance attacks the leisurely serenity of academia.

Even the most individualistic of persons—the musician, the artist, the writer—is dependent on the interplay and accommodation of many people. The musician can get nowhere without the producer, the concert hall, the ticket sellers, the advertising media, the record companies, the reviewers, and the tax accountants. Artists remain unknown without the system of galleries, museums, critics, markets, and collectors. Writers remain obscure without the help of publishing companies, phototypesetting and high-speed presses, reviewers, bookstores, and distribution centers.

Dealing with the human factors affecting an organization involves a complex of many factors and an almost infinite range of possible interplays between them. As in chess, amateurs see only one move at a time; masters see the chain of consequences many moves ahead. The really meaningful move is the move after the move after this one—the end consequence of a chain of actions and reactions.

chapter 33   Preparing for the consequences of success

I⊤ is a paradox of our times that the more any group advances in mastery of its own field, the more certain it is to get out of touch with the rest of the population. It becomes more complex, its knowledge becomes more intense, its interests more esoteric.

The vast and rapid sweep of change has made almost everything bigger, broader, and much more complicated.

a. Employment is provided much less on the farms and in small businesses and much more in huge corporate and government complexes.

b. Education is focused less on the local school board and superintendents and more on the state legislature and the federal government.

c. Religion is much less involved with attendance at the local church and much more involved with national organizations and international influence.

d. Government is less the local city hall and more the vast complex in Washington.

e.   Entertainment is less the family social or the local lodge, and more the instant experiencing with millions of others of suspense, thrills, skills, and dramatics via TV, the movies, and huge sports events.

All of these changes can be seen as the successes of the groups within these fields, yet all have created severe problems. In fact, most of the problems facing managements today are the results of their own successes.

a.   Colleges' problems would be minor if college degrees hadn't been made so desirable.
b.   The auto industry wouldn't be faced with castigation for air pollution, accidents, and junkers if cars hadn't become so desirable to everyone.
c.   The health care field wouldn't be faced with legislation to conscript medical services if there hadn't been such progress in what medicine can do for people.
d.   The utilities would have few problems if the demand for power hadn't grown so fast.
e.   Service problems on TV and appliances are the after-effect of the massive purchase of these products, as well as other problems.

Every plan should have in it provisions for meeting the problems that will result from its success—and for what should be done each step of the way to anticipate and attenuate them.

The contingencies of success

Suppose, for example, that a company plans to enter a new business with a newly developed product. Now it must plan for new financing, new plant capacity, a new work force, a new executive staff, a new sales and distribution system, new sources of materials, and related start-up requirements. It must make allowances for the added overhead costs, advertising and publicity budgets, and other needs.

This is a formidable battery of requirements. But it stops at the point where it is hoped the product will be a success. What about the needs if it does succeed?

a. Will it change the relations between the executives of various segments of the business?
b. Will it put a new load on the traffic, schools, and pollution levels in the area of the plant?
c. Will it change the company's relations with distributors and dealers?
d. Will it alter the attitude of the investment community and stockholders toward the company?
e. Will it lead the government to begin thinking the company is too big or that it has too large a share of its market?
f. Will it encounter the activist criticism of consumerists, safety groups, or those who criticize "creating unnecessary desires"?
g. Will the disposal of the product create new refuse problems?

A few years ago most of these would have been idle questions. Today they are the area in which the real and most knotty problems of management arise.

Now no planning can be complete unless it contains within it well-thought-out consideration of the consequences of the plan's success.

SECTION V Affecting the people factor

chapter 34   The real role of communication

THE ability to communicate complex thoughts is probably the single greatest factor that differentiates man from all other animals. It has made it possible to combine the capabilities and experience of millions of men for the benefit of each new individual. It has made the accomplishments and the wisdom of thousands of generations the cumulative heritage of each of us as we try to cope with the challenges of living experience. It has made possible a complex society that is tied together by many concepts we hold in common, while giving great status to the role of every individual.

And yet, most of the weaknesses and the failures in human society can be traced to our inexpertness in communication.

We have spent billions of dollars and the talents of hundreds of thousands of people to probe the mysteries of outer space, the ocean floor, and the invisible viruses. But there has been, even today, shockingly little systematic research into this vital area of communication that not only makes all other human explorations possible, but will determine whether the human experience will even continue.

It is essential that managers really understand what the com-

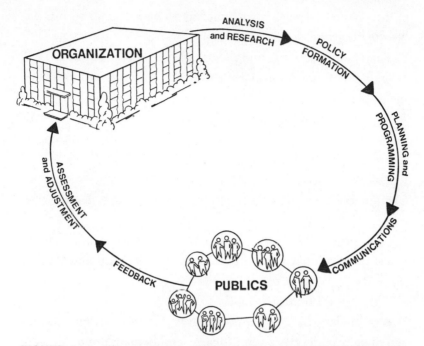

FIGURE 34.1.   Diagram of an optimum process in public relations. It is
continuous, not oriented to single events or objectives;
interacting, with each phase affecting the conception
and execution of every other phase; and *proportioned,*
with no one element (such as communications) predomi-
nating.

Source: Philip Lesly, ed. *Lesly's Public Relations Handbook.* © 1971, Prentice-
Hall, Inc.

munication process is. For generations there has been a gross
oversimplification that continues to bar the way to effectiveness.

It is best understood by diagramming the typical communication process of organizations.

The starting point is analysis and research to understand the
underlying conditions and the nature and leanings of the publics.

After that, policy determinations can be made, aimed at bringing the organization into confluence with the trends and leanings

of the publics, rather than attempting to buck them and inevitably meeting immovable resistance.

Then come planning and programming, which are carried out through communications efforts intended to reach and influence the publics.

Feedback from the publics is then picked up and assessed, followed by adjustments in the organization's awareness of its own role and its relationships to the publics.

This continuous process is a constant accommodation, a reconciliation between the organization and the groups it must deal with.

Like most other truisms of a past era that have proved to be inadequate in today's climate, the concept of communication as a two-way process is passé.

The organization is as much affected by what comes back to it from this loop of communication as it is by its own deliberations and objectives. Today's sophisticated and demanding publics are as much a moving force behind the interchange in communications as the organization itself.

The manager can no longer visualize himself as standing behind a microphone addressing his audiences. He must think instead of his being a part of a noisy crowd, in which he must gain a hearing on the basis of the merit of his message and the skill of his persuasiveness rather than of a superior position or a stronger voice.

chapter 35 Requirements for a successful communications program

THERE are four basic essentials in an effective communications effort. All of them must be executed expertly or nothing will be accomplished. Most managers tend to think in terms of one or two of them at most.

It is an anomoly that modern managers are quick to replace a four-year-old computer system with a later one and to trade in an airplane for a newer model; yet their practice of communications is still essentially the same as it was in the 19th century—in content, in style, and in techniques.

The four basic essentials are:

1. *Having something meaningful to say.*

Not being trained in the subtlties and nuances of communication, many managers instinctively approach the function on the basis of patterns carried over from earlier times. In previous eras, people tended to look up to authority and to draw much of their wisdom from the words of respected ministers, government lead-

ers, civic figures, and business tycoons. Now, of course, it is a rare
authority who is looked up to and listened to.

Only two generations ago speeches and literature were scarce.
The Chautauqua and the pamphlet represented for many people
entertainment, social life, and promise of advancement in this life
or the next. In that situation, statements or literature tended to
be welcomed. Speeches by great orators such as Robert Ingersoll
and William Jennings Bryan were carried around and declaimed
from the stages of schools, lodges, and meeting halls.

Today, of course, almost everyone feels inundated with messages clamoring for his attention. The individual, in defense of
his psyche, erects safety valves that shut out the great majority
of efforts to capture his attention and to move him.

To be meaningful today a communication must:

a.   Have direct concern for the audience, gauging its self-interest
and identifying it with the subject.
b.   Be new, fresh, or humorous—capable of being distinctive
from the torrents of other messages that fill each day.
c.   Cover the facts and background and then come to conclusions that the audience will also recognize as its logical
conclusion. It is no longer possible to project conclusions *at*
people; we can only try to arrive at the same conclusions together.

2. *Saying it the most effective way.*

The avalanche of literature, seminars, and other communications devoted to the art of communication has been predomi-
nantly in this area. It is as though the pearly phrase and the dulcet
tone were the essence of communication.

There is no doubt that the greatest weaknesses continue to be
the ponderous and turgid expressions that emanate from the great
majority of executives, teachers, government officials, and others.
Writers such as Rudolf Flesch (*The Art of Plain Talk, The Art*

of Readable Writing, etc.), Henry M. Boettinger (*Moving Mountains*), and John O. Morris (*Make Yourself Clear*) have impressed much of the management community with the pitfalls of poor writing and presentation. But, alas, thousands who are capable of mastering a course in data processing in four weeks show little progress from half a lifetime of exposure to the techniques of good expression.

As we shall see in Chapters 38–41, today's management communications continue to be full of bad practices. And while many managers are competent in expository writing, there are few indeed, since the late Clarence Randall, who have been masters of it.

Almost any message can be presented in a way that either repels the audience, rolls off its mental defenses without effect, or breaks through and influences the recipient.

One of the most difficult problems is that there are so many different types of verbal communication that management may have to employ:

a. Reports.

b. Sales presentations.

c. Presentations before security analysts.

d. Communications to stockholders.

e. Editorials in company publications.

f. Recruitment literature for college seniors.

g. Speeches before business organizations.

h. Testimony before Congressional hearings.

i. Speeches at anniversary and other celebrations.

j. Tough admonitions to staff members to "get on the ball." and a host of others.

The manager is rare who executes any one of these superbly; only an unusual artist in communicating—probably a specialist in mass communication with years of experience—is likely to be a master in all of them.

3. *Selecting the best means to get the message to the audience.*
In most organizations, there is an instinctive turning toward
the media that are available or those that staff members have had
training with. The manager without media training tends to look
to the controlled outlet, in which the message can be placed and
thrust before the audience: house organs, paid advertisements,
letters, bulletin boards. Staff people who once worked on newspapers tend to think of getting out a newspaper release. Those who
were employed by trade publications think of an announcement
story to the trade press.

Here again, the nuances and variations are multiple. A choice
of the means for conveying any message is likely to involve:

• *The nature and the frame of mind of the audience involved.*
Should the message be presented overtly from the management or indirectly? Most of the time, the choice will determine
whether the effort fails completely or has a good chance of
success.

• *The nature of the subject or issue involved.* Is it primarily
informational? Laden with emotional overtones? Striking at the
sense of security or self-worth of the audience?

• *Timing.* Should it reach the audience just before or just after
an increase in wages or dividends? Is there time to run it in the
monthly house organ or does every minute count?

• *Locale.* Is the audience all in one plant or community, or is
it dispersed in many places or throughout the country or, indeed,
the world?

• *What media are available?* House organs, advertisements, and
bulletin boards may come immediately to mind, but what about
publications, meetings, printed literature, publicity in newspapers or magazines, television or radio interviews, slidefilms or
motion pictures, seminars?

• *Is it important that the message reach the audience through a third party?* If visibility of the self-interest of the spokesmen will mean the message will probably be rejected, having it carried by respected publications or broadcasters (who are respected because they carry information that their judgment indicates is important and sound) may be the necessary channel.

• *Budget considerations.* How important is the objective in terms of budget availabilities? A notice on all bulletin boards, if it accomplishes the purpose, is a better choice than an expensive motion picture. An editorial by the president in the company publication that will be rejected because of its self-interest is expensive even though its cost is minimal.

Skill in selecting and using the media of communications is as vital a management function as orchestrating the many aspects of an organization's operations.

4. *Attaining receptivity by the audience.*

All efforts and skills are wasted if no motivation occurs at the receiving end.

Sensitivity to how people will respond, what turns them off, and what can move them is an art that, like other arts, can be partially learned but must be inherent.

Winston Churchill could have said, in his famous House of Commons speech in May 1940: "We're going to have a hard time of it, but if everyone will do his duty we will win." Instead he said: "I have nothing to offer but blood, toil, tears and sweat"; and he won the dogged resistance of an entire nation.

In 1950, playing a musical instrument was considered passé in the United States, going the same way as quilting parties and taffy pulls. People could have been approached to give their children music lessons because it would be fun or because it would advance them socially. But parents then were becoming painfully aware that problems in child behavior were becoming endemic. So the

American Music Conference issued a script that was carried on most of America's radio stations calling attention to the fact that things were too easy for their kids and suggesting: "Give your child a challenge." The logic and the merits of having youngsters need to discipline themselves and master a talent in order to create their pleasures won over countless educators and parents, and a boom in musical instruments was under way.

chapter 36 Three phases of a communications program

THE communications functions of an organization usually break down broadly into two categories:

1. Preparation and dissemination of information that is primarily internal—intended for staff, employees, stockholders, and others having a direct relationship with the organization.

2. External communication, involving primarily dealings with communications media not under the control of the organization.

The second category constitutes most of the mass-communications aspects. And for most organizations, there are three elements of this mass-communications program:

1. Responding to the requests of communications media and others. This is a passive, service function. It calls for having information and sources organized, then conscientiously responding to the initiatives of those to be served.

2. Arranging for press coverage and dissemination of information on events and the routine output of the organization. This calls for constant awareness of the news-making functions within the organization and routine channels of contact with the media; but it is also essentially a passive function.

3. Initiative in stimulating the media and others to achieve the organization's desired purposes. This calls for creative development of ideas and concepts; maintaining and nurturing respected liaison with hundreds of important media people and writers; and constant initiative in making them receptive to the organization's ideas and materials.

It is common in the communications field to concentrate on what is responsive and comes easily, such as meeting the requests of press people; handling publicity for events and tangible documents; developing and mailing "handouts" to minor or intermediate media such as farm publications, company magazines, small newspapers and radio stations; and noncontroversial public-service material that is readily acceptable by the media but accomplishes comparatively little for the organization.

On the other hand, the greatest need in almost all organizations is to focus concentrated effort on the knotty problems. Because these are knotty problems, it is more difficult to get an audience and response from the media on them. They involve complex concepts and ideas, rather than simple facts and specifics such as a skin disorder or overweight. And they are wrapped up in the complexities of the organization.

It is curious how many managers who recognize that a successful sales program requires concentration on initiative fail to recognize that the same is true in a successful mass-communications effort. Staff size and budget often are established on the basis of what is needed to deal with the first two phases cited here, with the result that the vital initiative phase is always short-changed.

Even when allotments are made for the initiative functions, it is common to call on the communications staff to account for every detail in the two passive areas, even though that requires putting aside the difficult and the creative aspects of initiative.

Good management of the communications program calls for

emphasizing the potentially most productive aspects—the results of initiative—and leaving ample time and resources that are not committed to the routine functions so the initiative functions can have sufficient scope.

chapter 37 Conditions that affect the communication process

In previous chapters we have explored four basic essentials in an effective communications effort and three phases of the primary activities in a mass-communication program.

With these in mind, there are six aspects of the communication process that will determine what happens with the audience of a mass-communication program:

1. *A predisposition by the intended recipient of the communication, or at least neutrality.*

This predisposition is a composite of his heritage and his outlook on life, plus all the information and impressions about the subject of the communication that have accumulated throughout his lifetime.

A completely written communication from a copper producing company about proposed legislation that would severely alter its ability to operate a smelter will scarcely be received in the same way by these five members of its intended audience:

a. A graduate of Yale who lives in Greenwich and whose family has long enjoyed good dividends from holdings in that company's stock.

b. An executive in a firm manufacturing electrical appliances who is concerned about having to close down a major part of his operations if the shortage of copper wire becomes more acute.

c. A student attending a state university on a work-study program whose family has worked in copper mines for three generations, and who is strongly motivated toward upward mobility.

d. A leader in an environment-protection organization who believes that preservation of the atmosphere demands a sharp curtailment in the production and consumption of most goods.

e. A professor of sociology who wrote his Ph.D. thesis on the problems of families who live in mining towns.

A major consideration in many mass-communication programs, therefore, must be an assessment of the predisposition or lack of it among various segments of the intended audience.

2. *An innate propensity by all people to believe what is comforting to one's psyche or that shields it from guilt or fear.*

". . . people tend to select, organize, and interpret stimuli in line with existing motives; their thoughts and memories are similarly channeled and modified according to what is important or gratifying to think and remember," it is pointed out by Berelson and Steiner.[1]

Even so intelligent and objective a man as the late Edward R. Murrow (a heavy smoker)—less than a year before his death from lung cancer and while he was suffering from a persistent cough —expressed scorn for the findings that linked cigarette smoking with the incidence of lung cancer.

The fact that at least 75 percent of all drivers still refuse to use the seat belts installed in their cars, despite massive communications efforts, is due to their blocking out of their reasoning all information and arguments in favor of buckling up.

3. *The basic needs of the individual, such as sense of worth, group acceptance, self-admiration, security, skill, knowledge, and power.*

Every master persuader and every demagogue has known instinctively how to play on the eagerness of the individual to accept what he hears that contributes to his self-esteem or other emotional bents.

Everyone is surrounded by an invisible screen of defense against an inundation of messages. Associating a message with a thought that captures the individual's ego-related needs is one of the surest ways to break through.

4. *The basic need for harmony between the individual's needs and desires, and the demands and pressures on him, including conscience and other forces.*

The person inherently moves toward acceptance of what enhances harmony and shields himself from what might create dissonance within him.

The devout Roman Catholic who would face a crisis of dissonance if he accepted the arguments in favor of abortion not only rejects the arguments but rallies his psyche in defense of his beliefs. He may be motivated to act oppositely to the intention of the person seeking to persuade him to support legal abortion.

5. *The fidelity of the message.*

Does it reach the recipient in the shape in which it was sent? This involves the physics of transmission—sound waves, light waves, and so on.

It involves the clarity of both transmission and reception, including such matters as whether accents are recognizable or colors are clear.

It is strongly affected by the diction and tone of the speaker and by the hearing acuity and vision of the receiver.

It involves the semantics of the situation: do the sender and the auditor give the same precise meaning to the words and symbols? "Freedom" means entirely different things to the lifer in prison, the inhabitant of a black slum, a teenager who balks at restrictions on dating and use of marijuana, a teacher who wants to select his own reading sources for the classroom, a husband who feels rejected by the frigidity of his wife, and the business manager who is confronted with rigid regulation of many aspects of his operations.

One of the most serious and most common of all errors in communication is failure to stand "in the shoes" of the intended auditor when composing the message, to be as sure as possible that his interpretation will be anticipated and accounted for in what the speaker says and how he says it.

6. *The skill and experience of the communicator—the overriding factor in all communications efforts.*

Masterful skills can work wonders; ineptness or even average ability can create directly opposite results.

Many managers who seek out the finest attorney available when a major law suit is looming, or who insist on the best surgeon when an operation is necessary, consider it adequate to assign "a writer"—anyone whose experience record indicates he has written things—to plan and compose major communications materials.

The inadequacy of this approach is indicated by the fact that the public relations field is supposedly made up of specialists in mass communication; and yet it is perhaps the most misunderstood and one of the most maligned of all fields of endeavor in the United States.

Communications materials that are "almost right" are as undesirable as an "almost right" 23-foot leap over a 25-foot chasm.

chapter 38 Common ineptitudes in communication programs

Many organizations are losing their battle for public opinion because they have the wrong programs and use the wrong technique.

Some common flaws in programs intended to meet attacks include:

1. *Concentrating on answering criticisms.*

It is necessary . . . but seldom enough to win. It's like meeting the question "Have you stopped beating your wife?" by protesting that you don't beat her. You have to take her out in public and let her be seen unblemished and happy. It is necessary to anticipate what criticisms may be coming to be sure you can show your case to advantage—and to show it before someone attacks.

2. *Working to "get our story across."*

This is trying to communicate *at* people. But people ignore messages that aren't on their personal wave length. Recently leaders in autos, oil, banking, and medicine have described their communications needs as getting people to know what their fields are doing—one-directional communication attuned to the desires of the sender, rather than the interests of the audience.

3. *Failing to organize the facts and basic case.*

At this writing, one of America's greatest industries—under attack from many directions for months—still has no concise "backgrounder" document that cites the underlying forces, marshalls pertinent facts, and presents them from the point-of-view of the public's interest.

4. *Missing the principles of persuasion.*

Writing is heavy-handed. Self-interest shouts so loud it drowns out the merits of the case.

5. *Failing to coordinate battle forces.*

Work on Congressmen and government bureaus takes one tack, public statements another, and word to employees a third. Communications can't be kept from interflowing today. Contradictions destroy credibility.

6. *Thinking is too inbred.*

A group of insiders alone has trouble getting into tune with outside publics.

Every manager must seek out ways to break up tendencies toward insularity and like-minded thinking.

He must consciously put creative, pattern-breaking minds on his team.

He must listen to uncomfortable reminders that constant uncertainty about the way things are is part of the inescapable makeup of responsible management.

He must accustom himself to having his way of expressing things and his most comfortable instincts for doing it reviewed by objective and expert outsiders—retaining his prerogative as a manager to decide, but keeping his mind open to the outside viewpoint.

chapter 39 Anti-communication: Art over meaning

DESPITE the constant attention managers devote to the importance of good communication, there are a number of current trends in communication that interfere with communicating. They are really *anti*-communication.

In this and the next three chapters we will examine some of the most common and most serious types of anti-communication —efforts to communicate that not only fail but are self-defeating or even counterproductive.

One of the most damaging is the tendency to reach so hard for effect that the message is lost or distorted.

a. Type treatments defy legibility. They repel the audience instead of communicating.
b. Multiple, repeated fast cuts in films thwart the audience's efforts to make out what's shown.
c. Multimedia presentations usually drown the audience in impressions, but communicate too little.
d. Color combinations are chosen deliberately by artists to affront the eye, but make the subject or words illegible.

FIGURE 39.1. A number of treatments of type emphasize "art" at the expense of communication. The illegibility of some is compounded by the use of clashing or overlapping colors.

e. Logotypes that convey no real meaning have appeared like a flurry of snowflakes—each different, but all adding up to a pile of slush in the mind of the public.

Since the purpose of communications material is to communicate, there are a few rules that not even today's art-oriented genius can violate:

a. It must meet the needs of the audience.
b. It must be as clear to the audience as possible.
c. It must be simple . . . precise . . . concise.
d. It should be attractive, to get the audience's attention. But the most attractive thing possible is something the viewer recognizes has meaning for him—and that meaning must be recognizable as soon as possible.
e. Then—if all these other needs are met—it is helpful if it creates an impression in addition to its inherent meaning. But impression for the sake of impression is phony and fails.

chapter 40　Anti-communication: The snobbery of jargon

ANOTHER form of anti-communication that is growing is jargon. Segments of our society are being separated by the languages they create.

Special terminologies are problem enough when they result from increasing specialization. Practitioners of each field have to give their specialty more attention, and so decrease their attention to others. As groups pay less attention to each other, they also develop more esoteric jargon and become harder for others to understand, breeding suspicion and confusion.

But increasingly there is an added factor: snobbery. People want to make sure others recognize they are on a different level, so they deliberately develop jargon that sets them apart.

There are many examples, such as "motivational deprivation" (for laziness); "an interrelated collectivity" (for group); "conceptualize" (imagine); "aversive control techniques," "optokinetic perception," "morphological projections," "probabilistic exploratory forecasting," "extrapolation of time-series on a phenomenological basis."

When a term becomes known to many others, it is often

173

changed, such as "dementia praecox" becoming "schizophrenia" and "infantile paralysis" becoming "poliomyelitis."

Stuart Chase pointed out that the type of language used by various groups influences and dictates their thought processes, behavior, and attitude toward life. Different kinds of language tend to make groups different in outlook and therefore are divisive.

Henry A. Barnes pointed out:

All "inside" languages begin with a group's desire to foster efficiency. It is only when the group loses or discards its initial motivation to serve the general public that the "outside" language falls into discard. The "inside" tongue now develops in direct proportion to the group's new inclination to isolate itself and deceive or confuse outsiders.

Language is supposed to be a bridge between people or between an organization and people. Jargon—especially when motivated by snobbery or a yen for status—digs chasms.

As the population becomes more and more segmented, there is a greater tendency for everyone to develop a vocabulary that is foreign to growing segments of the public. Even within a given organization, where managers with various specializations must deal with each other and converse regularly, there is always the need to restate one's expressions so they will be grasped by others. The accountant, the lawyer, the researcher, and the production man—while they all deal with the same company's activities—can readily fall into the use of jargon that is foreign to each other.

This means that the communications of every organization that must reach outside groups—and especially when there are a number of diverse groups involved—can benefit from the participation of an expert who is both objective and experienced in using language that is universally understood.

chapter 41 Anti-communication: The lost art of writing

AMERICA today has an explosion of communications—and is having more trouble communicating than ever.

A national study financed by the federal government showed that "nine-year-olds show almost no command of the basic writing mechanics." Among 86,000 children aged 9, 13, and 17 in 2,500 schools in every part of the country, plus 8,000 adults, only five had a really good command of the English language.

This confirms that Johnny not only can't read, he can't write. And the breakdown in communication means few people have the basis for sound thinking.

Here are some clues to the underlying factors:

1. Children are not disciplined to read by learning the words, but do it phonically. As a result, they don't visualize words or constructions. They don't really recognize words or how ideas are put together. Whatever sounds close is considered okay.

2. Meaning is destroyed in many ways: exaggeration ("revolutionary" for "modified," "superstar" for "good performer," "unique" for "unusual," "fascist" for "disciplined"); jargon; euphemisms ("activism" for "assault," "socially disoriented" for

"criminally inclined"); distortions (a scholarship based on need, not scholarship).

3. Stress on audio-visual media makes it easy to feel educated and informed on a diet of superficial material. McLuhan fostered this by declaring the printed word dead, long before audio-visual media can provide the depth and variety needed.

4. The antidiscipline attitude seen in other aspects of life spreads to include lack of care in using language.

5. Politicians and welfarists complain about the "injustice" of judging people who use bastardized language "because they don't know any better." They don't require everyone to learn English, but accept a native tongue as "equal" even if its users can't cope with our society's needs. They foster anti-communication.

Making nothing perfectly clear

It has often been said that clear writing is impossible without clear thinking. You have to be sure of your ideas to express them so others will understand. But it's not widely recognized that if you write turgidly, your thinking will become turgid.

Modern managers often try so hard to skirt the touchiness of what they say, they bog down in murkiness. Their convoluted thinking process then muddies their own thinking. Clear writing is essential for clear thought on both sides of the communications equation—the writer and the reader.

George Orwell (*1984, Animal Farm*) was not only a social prophet. He also foresaw the present misuses of the English language. In 1945 he said: "The whole tendency of modern prose is away from concreteness."

Ideas should never be set in concrete, but the more concretely they can be expressed, the more clearly the audience will perceive them.

Orwell attacked clichés, ponderous phrases (*exhibit a tendency* for *tend*), pomposity, and vagueness. He set down this rule that ought to be standard for everyone who seeks to communicate:

A scrupulous writer, in every sentence that he writes, will ask himself at least four questions, thus: What am I trying to say? What words will express it? What image or idiom will make it clearer? Is this image fresh enough to have an effect? And he will probably ask himself two more: Could I put it more shortly? Have I said anything that is avoidably ugly? [1]

We would add this as No. 1 in the list of key questions: *Whom am I trying to reach and what is that audience's orientation?*

Many people today follow the precept that emphasis on the precise use of words, correct sentence structure, and the rules of grammar is an eccentricity of "purists." If a message includes what's intended to be said, they feel, what difference do the "niceties" make? Ironically, many of those who feel that "almost right" is good enough for conveying ideas are sticklers for precision in their computerized and measured attention to tangibles.

Aside from the countless instances of misunderstanding that are due to unclear writing, there is a vast difference in effectiveness between pedestrian language and masterful expression.

Some people use words like underwear, merely to cover the subject. Others use them like lingerie, to present it at its best.

Good use of language is one of the greatest achievements of civilization. It has made all other achievements possible. The concurrence of breakdown in our society and breakdown in use of the language is no coincidence.

chapter 42 Anti-communication: The lure of idea ads

MANAGERS are inherently geared to tangibles and action. They want visible signs of something being done.

Their big current problems are the hostile or indifferent attitudes of groups: consumerists, conservationists, intellectuals, labor, minorities, youth, government, women's organizations. So managers are tempted to use the most visible form of communication—institutional advertising.

Ads that "tell your story" are alluring. They permit presenting exactly what you want, to exactly the audience you select, under exactly the conditions you choose.

These are the very reasons institutional advertising is probably the most misused and wasteful form of communication.

The fact it is so attractive to the communicator means that, unless great care and skill are used, it's likely to "turn off" the intended recipient. He balks at even exposing his psyche to obvious and expensive efforts to sway him, so often these efforts backfire. Any discrepancy is grasped at; any stretched fact is made the basis of attack on the advertiser.

No volume of institutional ads will get a viewpoint across unless

THE $66 BILLION MISTAKE

Dangerous curve ahead

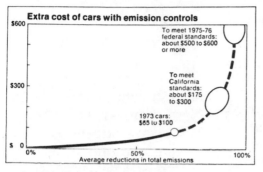

Extra cost of cars with emission controls

To meet 1975-76 federal standards: about $500 to $600 or more

To meet California standards: about $175 to $300

1973 cars: $65 to $100

0% — Average reductions in total emissions — 50% — 100%

$0 / $300 / $600

The Administrator of the Environmental Protection Agency earlier this month proposed a plan to reduce driving in the Los Angeles basin a whopping 82% during the summer months, beginning in 1975, and to impose other severe burdens on motorists there.

He made it clear that he was simply complying with a court order to come up with something that would —at least on paper—meet federally prescribed air quality standards by 1977. He candidly expressed "serious reservations as to the feasibility" of his drastic proposals. And, according to the press, "he indicated that the public must decide 'through the political process' whether other measures—such as mass transit—or revision of the law to provide more time or reduced standards should be sought."

Admittedly, Los Angeles has unique air pollution problems that cannot be solved by 1977—though that city's air pollution control officials believe a solution by the early 1980s *is* possible. In any event, the Los Angeles dilemma dramatizes the hazards of trying to achieve more than is possible within an arbitrarily short time span.

The only way completely to eliminate automotive emissions in Los Angeles or anywhere else would be to do away with the automobile itself. Since neither this nor what the EPA Administrator proposed for the Los Angeles basin is practical or desirable, the question is: What

percentage reduction *should* we aim for? By what date? And at what cost?

Where does the country stand today? As the result of control devices and changes in engine design in the past 12 years, 1973-model cars are engineered to reduce emissions of the three harmful pollutants—hydrocarbons, carbon monoxide, and nitrogen oxides—to an average of 66% below pre-control cars.

Total air pollution from automobiles is already on the way down and will drop further as older cars with less efficient controls are scrapped.

But the federal government has mandated the reduction of emissions by 1976-model cars to an average of 95% below pre-control levels. These standards would be so difficult to achieve with today's proven technology that they would be very expensive to the public.

There is, however, a satisfactory alternative—a set of technically and economically feasible standards proposed by the state of California. They would reduce emissions of the three main pollutants to an average of 83% below pre-control levels.

Meeting the California standards could cost Americans about $34 billion over the 10 years beginning in 1976. We estimate meeting the federal standards could cost roughly $100 billion over the same decade. The difference between these

two figures could be a $66 billion mistake.

Higher initial cost of the emission-control hardware accounts for much of the $66 billion difference. The chart shows how sharply this cost rises as emission reductions go beyond what California recommended.

Additionally, cars meeting the federal standards could consume about 15% more gasoline per mile than cars meeting the California standards, and would require more and costlier maintenance and tune-ups.

To give you an idea of what is involved, $66 billion would:
☐ Buy 44 rapid-transit systems like the BART system in San Francisco.
☐ Roughly equal annual U.S. expenditures for all health and medical care ($67 billion in 1970).
☐ More than pay for all new private and public housing construction in this country for two years (1970 total: $30 billion).
☐ Nearly pay the total cost of all types of education in the U.S., at all levels, for a year (1970 total: $69 billion).

Companies in various industries are developing emission-control systems and testing them for durability and economy. Some of these systems offer exciting possibilities for reducing emissions to very low levels. But the most critical element is time—time to test various devices and systems for thousands of miles and to engineer the systems for mass production.

In view of all this, we believe:
☐ The Environmental Protection Agency should grant a one-year extension on the federal standards.
☐ The Congress should re-examine the Clean Air Act as it relates to automobiles.

Meanwhile we, and you, would have to be out of our minds to let a possible $66 billion mistake go unchallenged.

FIGURE 42.1.   An advertisement that seeks to persuade the audience through a long treatment of the advertiser's viewpoint on a controversial and emotional issue.

Is somebody throwing you a curve

Let's get things straight... to help save lives on your highways.

Disregarding your needs as a motorist, certain zealous groups have taken aim at highways... ignoring the fact that highways engineered to modern safety standards help save lives. Yet 700,000* miles of America's roads and highways, including some *you* may drive on, are far below modern standards. Built many years ago, they are not adequate for to-day's traffic needs.

Sharp curves need straightening. Narrow lanes need widening. Steep grades need leveling. Around urban centers, special lanes for commuter express buses can keep people moving.

This does not mean building new roads. It means improving existing roads. For more on making present highways safer and more efficient, write:

The Road Information Program, Inc., 525 School St., S.W., Washington, D.C. 20024.

Your highways. You've got a lot riding on them.

FIGURE 42.2. An advertisement by the highway industry that seeks to combat arguments for diverting funds from highways to advancing public transit systems.

* Source: *1972 National Highway Needs Report.* Does not include local streets.

it is presented from the orientation of the recipient. If it can't have that orientation, the case is probably untenable.

Those shown here are examples of such ads written with the audience's orientation in mind. Both discipline and skilled writing are needed to combine that orientation and the objective of the advertiser.

Approaches most likely to have the audience's orientation include:

1. Interesting *facts* that are pertinent to the self-interest of the reader or audience. People affected by a strike are concerned about the facts offered by both sides. Issues such as the need for energy and the advancement of mass transit are other examples.

2. Tips or authoritative information that perform a *service* for the reader. Many people will read carefully an ad about how to protect against burglary or how to provide a good diet with low-cholesterol foods.

3. Information that clarifies a problem that has been perplexing the reader, such as how to get his car serviced without delay and frustration, or the *full* background (not just "the other side") behind charges that have been leveled against an institution or a company he has an interest in.

Even if the message gains an audience and is accepted, only those who by interest or training are receptive to the message will then be influenced by it.

Overt messages, where the organization and its purpose are visible, often do not change attitudes. More realistic goals are providing the basis for knowledge where little exists, and "inoculating" the audience against virulent accusations that come later.

chapter 43 The receptivity of the audience

THE posture of the audience is a vital factor in other forms of communication besides advertising.

Shifting and molding people's ideas is far different from selling them something they are disposed toward. Direct advertising and selling can be effective when people are predisposed to listen, but only subtle and indirect persuasion can work when they are negative or indifferent.

As the late Pierre Martineau said:

Almost all adults . . . resent direct suggestion. Actually, it is an attack on their ego integrity, telling them to do this and that, shattering their beliefs and prejudices. . . . Indirect suggestion avoids clashing with the other individual's system of beliefs, which is his self.

All of us have had the experience of seeing an idea of ours violently rejected by another only to find that some time later the person had adopted our idea as if it had come from his own thinking. When he can feel that the idea came from his own thinking, he is far more likely to follow it.[1]

And Rex F. Harlow points out that:

People distrust a person or an organization with an obvious ax to grind. They resist messages that smack of selfish propaganda. They dislike exaggeration and boasting. In most situations an indirect content and an indirect approach tend to win more acceptance and support of an idea or a cause than a hard-hitting content and a direct-attack approach.[2]

In addition, in most cases the person selects the media to which he really exposes himself. Appearance of a message in a medium to which he has elected to expose himself predetermines a likely disposition toward at least recognizing and considering that message.

This is increasingly a vital factor in weighing the comparative value of *discretionary* media exposure (editorial material in newspapers and magazines, broadcast content of TV and radio, theatrical motion pictures, books) and *imposed* media exposure (advertisements, TV and radio commercials, literature not requested by the recipient, commercial motion pictures, propaganda speeches).

Without willing exposure by selection of the medium, many people cannot be reached by many messages, regardless of how much is spent or how massive the efforts to impose the message on them.

chapter 44 The need for many channels of communication

In our present complex society, with its multiform media, establishing an idea in the public mind calls for the use of many different channels.

If the idea of owning a boat is expressed a dozen times by one's teen-age son, for instance, it is quite different from having 12 different respected people, in a dozen different situations and circumstances, talk enthusiastically about the fun and excitement of boating.

When a multiple combination of impressions impinges on one's attention, the feeling is created that the idea is all-pervading, that it is "the thing to do." It therefore has considerably greater influence.

The same number of messages are likely to be far more effective if they are directed through many channels—newspapers, radio commentators, television programs, inclusion in motion pictures, word-of-mouth discussion, club meetings, and others—than repeatedly through the same means.

It is no longer likely that successful communication can be confined to a company newspaper, or just advertisements in the local press, or any other one or two outlets. Public relations to be effective must be as versatile and as all-encompassing of communications channels as the available resources and talents will permit.

Just 50 years ago the world of communication was simple and confined. In the United States, three wire services, some magazines, books, and a few major newspapers constituted the key channels of communication. The educated public that exposed itself to ideas or took a part in events was a small fraction of the population. Under these conditions, one staged event or one article in a magazine could alter public opinion.

Today we are experiencing an explosion of the scope that influencing of public opinion must cover. Besides the wire services and major newspapers, there are many more magazines, hundreds of newsletters, plus the multiplying forces of television, radio, sound and TV cassettes, motion pictures, and mass-distributed books.

A majority of the population represents the public to be reached, and it is educated, diffuse, and skeptical.

Except for an extremely rare occasion such as the first landing on the moon or the assassination of President Kennedy, no one event achieves general recognition immediately.

People must be reached by many channels, over a period of time, in the contexts of many diverse outlooks and windows on the world.

chapter 45 Dealing with the activist media

For a whole network of reasons, the nature of the communications media has changed in the past generation—not only technologically, but in orientation and effect. The change is both the result and the cause of ferments in our society.

In many ways, mass communication has progressed and improved more than any other element of modern living. Its impact has been vastly increased and is now dominant in determining what course events shall take.

What now goes into the press and over the air is largely determined by the bent of creative staffs. Creative people are, by definition, sensitive—and this often means they are critical of all about them, confronted by a world that puts greater store on solid (they would say, stolid) virtues and achievements than on their valued intangibles.

As Dr. Donald W. MacKinnon of the Institute of Personality Assessment and Research at the University of California, Berkeley, says: "There is the necessity in the creative person for a certain amount of what the poets have called 'divine discontent.'"

The ferment of discontent with established patterns is also traceable to the personal history of many media people.

On finishing school, they often found that established businesses and institutions were largely closed to the children of families not yet established. Accordingly, the women and non-WASPs who got college training and found the "establishment" barring them turned to avenues that were open—the media, as well as government, labor unions, social work, schools and colleges. These institutions, then, became largely staffed with well-educated, dedicated, antiestablishment personnel.

In turning from the establishment, they also in many cases turned from the competitive system it represented to them and developed rejection and scorn for the gross "practical" world.

Where the "media baron" who controlled voices of opinion in the past tended to be biased in favor of the status quo, many of the creative people of media today automatically favor anything that attacks it. In fact, there is a strong tendency on the part of some journalists to make over the world, and not just deal with events and interpretations of the news, as described in "The Reporter as Activist: A Fourth Revolution in Journalism."[1]

Competition for audiences and, even more, for advertising support becomes constantly fiercer.

First radio and then TV heated up the competitive pressure. Costs of TV demand that audiences be vast so advertising rates can be vaster.

Mass magazines find it hard to demonstrate their reason for existence in a world of TV, now in full color. *Collier's, The Saturday Evening Post, Look,* and *Life* have left monuments to the growing bitterness of competition for the audience.

Newspapers—even where there is a city-wide monopoly—find it harder to hold readers' attention and to keep advertising dollars ahead of rising costs. The pressure to grasp for attention intensifies.

All of these factors have shifted many media from their stance as reporters of the world scene to being activist protaganists in it. Learning to deal with them defensively and yet to utilize them as channels to the public is one of the most difficult challenges now facing managers. In later chapters we shall explore what managers need to do to meet these challenges.

chapter 46   Misuses of the past

THE past is one of the greatest casualties of the change that has occurred in how things develop in our society.

When change occurred gradually, and usually in only one or a few areas at one time, reasonable projections could be made of trend lines on the basis of past patterns of development. By looking at which traits and training had created outstanding business leaders, authors, or other talented people, a reasonable assumption could be made of the best way to prepare young people for success in these fields. A whole profession of chartists based its role of being able to predict the future of stock market actions on the historical market movements over a period of generations. Even projections of the need for police forces was based on past patterns of criminal activity.

One of the most significant of the concepts based on coping with the future by studying the past was the development of business education.

This took two forms:

1. The most prestigious of the graduate schools of business has based its operations on the "case method." This presumes that through intensive study of what has occurred in some organizations at some time in the past, and by exploring and discussing

the ramifications of that case, a person will become trained in how to cope with similar problems in his future responsibilities.

2. It is also presumed that the course of training and disciplines that has produced successful managers in the past will most probably produce the business leaders of the future.

Thus, despite the fact that for some years the really crucial problems facing many managers have been in the intangible areas of the human climate, few of the graduate schools of business in the United States have so much as one course that deals with this area. There is an occasional lecturer who explains for an hour what he does in public affairs, public relations, or corporate communications. Occasionally some reference is made during the process of plumbing a case study to the fact that human attitudes must be considered. But the mass of students continue to be processed on the presumption that they will be best trained by following the same pattern as the business students of fully a generation ago.

Combing the past for answers

This pursuit of the outmoded practice of extrapolating future plans out of past patterns combined with the training that many managers receive leads to a widespread urge to comb the past in making plans. This is part of the urge to pin down all possible factors into tangibles and to make accurate tangible predictions.

This situation is the source of much of the miscalculation —especially in the areas of consumerism, minority relations, government relations, and environmental problems—that besets managers of American organizations.

As part of this plumbing of the past, a great deal of attention is devoted to determining what presumably have been the attitudes, the prejudices, and the proclivities of various publics. Market and opinion research are looked at as "fact" finding.

But in our fast-moving times, any reading based on what people used to think or even what they think now is likely to be out of date by the time any new action or communication can take effect.

Studies of how people responded to questionnaires a few months ago or how they reacted to "similar" events previously can be only clues to even their present attitudes and potential responses, not charts of what they will be in the future. For example, readings on the public's attitude toward bigger government involvement and funding of various social programs made in 1971 proved to be far off base by the time of President Nixon's landslide re-election in 1972.

It is vital to lead the target by anticipating what the climate of attitudes will be when the action or communication will take effect. To base plans and communications on what has gone before, or even what is occurring now, is to base one's future on *re*action rather than action.

Polls and surveys can prove very effective in dealing with non-emotion-laden subjects such as like or dislike for a proposed new product or the possible interest in receiving a new magazine. However, when the management of a trade association, government bureau, or corporation looks for answers to what public reaction will be to emotion-laden matters—such as locating a new highway or invoking a school-integration program—findings from a survey often prove ephemeral.

Every message directed to every audience is unique in its time and impact. The individual's frame of mind is different from that he was in when some previous message was aimed at him. His response to a *hypothetical* question may vary greatly from his reaction to a *reality* that looms as a factor in his life.

The importance to him of each message is a vital element. So it is not possible to predict the response to any message on the basis of what the response has been to any previous message. A notable example was the reaction to President Nixon's announcement of Phase I of the wage-and-price freeze. There was no possibility of predicting the response by looking at opinion polls that gave previous responses of the public on even somewhat related matters.

All types of information and intelligence are helpful grist for the manager's judgment. The past is a mine of vital facts and wisdom, and the wise executive learns his history and past patterns of success. Readings on public responses and surveys of its attitudes can help if they are used as such grist and not as substantive proof. The past is prologue—a source of clues to what lies ahead—rather than a script for future performance.

All the grist that goes into decisions involving the human climate must be weighed and positioned by the sensitivity, the experience, and the judgment of skilled professionals. There is no effective substitute yet—including the attitudes and actions of the past—for the honed intelligence of the exceptional human mind.

SECTION VI How to manage the human climate

chapter 47 The role of the manager

ALTHOUGH the bulk of the strategy, planning, and execution of a human-climate program will be the responsibility of the professionals in this field—both staff and outside consultants—the foundation for it lies with the top management of the organization.

Management, either by their action or inaction, determine whether the organization's human climate will engulf them haphazardly or be managed.

Management—by their decisions on what their policy shall be, their selection of experts and staff, the importance they give to the program, and the budget they allot—will largely determine the program's ultimate effectiveness.

And to a considerable extent, management must be involved in the program. They must participate in and decide on the questions of policy that arise continually. They must at times take an overt role, in making statements or public appearances, or in representing the visual identification of the organization.

There are three essentials for effectively managing an organization's human climate:

1. Recognition of the importance of this vital function and

determination to conduct it successfully. That is the responsibility of the manager. Increasingly, good management of any organization includes establishing this function as basic to everything it does.

2. Planning the structure of the program and its coordination into the organization's total operation. That is the joint responsibility of the management and the best available experts in mass communication. These may be staff personnel, outside specialists, or a combination of the two.

3. Carrying out the program. That should be assigned to the experts, but must involve the management actively and must follow management's guidelines.

Many managers who by heritage and training are oriented toward wrestling with the tangible operations of the organization tend to shy away from devoting their time to an area that eludes their grasp and requires an investment of thought and attention from a busy schedule. However, there are few managers who can count on being able to master the tangible aspects of their operations unless they include attaining command of the human-climate factors.

A good manager is dedicated to being in command of the factors affecting his organization, rather than being overrun by them. Increasingly, human factors are critical for the future of every organization. And the only way to be in command of the future is to help create the future human climate.

Yet much less than 1 percent of business' resources are now devoted to this need.

Nevertheless, increasing attention is being given to social audits of all organizations, based on the level of their relationships with their publics. These are guidelines. Investment of time and resources in active programs to manage the human climate more and more becomes a major requirement, rather than an extra nicety.

chapter 48 Analyzing the organization's position

A hard-headed analysis of underlying factors, made before plans are developed, is vital to the success of any program aimed at managing the human climate.

This analysis should incorporate an assessment of the past, the trends, and the present, but must include other factors as well.

• A broad view of all the interlocking trends, actions of other organizations, and so on.

• A reading of where various trends seem to be going, together with a reading on the projected course of the organization itself.

Typical key points to be covered include:

1. Are the objectives the right ones for now? Are they really obtainable, or wishful thinking?

Here is an adapted quotation from a report to a large organization:

Events in this field have rushed on, while the organization has been absorbed in keeping up with its own affairs. . . . To a considerable extent, communications functions have accumulated, rather than been planned. As a result, there is too little relationship between the climate of attitudes that now engulf it and the priorities of the organization in dealing with this climate.

2. What are the attitudes and underlying forces that affect whatever the organization will do or say?

Assess the entire cosmos in which the organization functions: internal conditions and plans; the industry it is in; the social trends in the locality, nationally, and internationally; the attitudes and practices of the media to be dealt with, and so on.

3. What are the specific obstacles? Is there a political barrier, such as solid entrenchment of opposition in a strong bloc of Congress? Is there a prejudice against the organization that logic and information will not dispel?

Planning may have to work around these, rather than attempt to beat them down.

4. What are the special opportunities?

Gearing to a trend or appetite can be as productive in climate-building as in new products.

5. What are present activities and how do they measure up against these criteria and conditions? Are they all closely related to the objectives? Are they oriented to the viewpoint of the audience? Are they visible and dramatic in this age of visibility?

6. What are others doing: allies, opponents, others whose functions will compete for attention or affect what may happen?

7. Is emphasis placed on leading the target—on establishing the climate of attitudes in the future, rather than responding to what has happened to date?

8. Is the chain reaction of various activities being considered?

9. Have allowances been made for the specific personalities, politics, and peculiarities of the situation?

Plans and activities that do not take into account the organization's traits are likely to fail. In one company the chief executive may be outgoing, articulate, and eager for respect; in another, he may resist anything that puts him into the limelight.

10. What resources are available—budgets, manpower, allies? If new needs are demonstrated, can resources be obtained? If not, can priorities be shifted so some "sacred cows" will be eliminated?

chapter **49**   **Planning**

As in statecraft, politics, and military affairs, the overwhelming majority of participants in mass-communications efforts deal with day-to-day execution of *techniques*.[1]

A smaller percentage is responsible for the *tactics* that set the pattern for technicians. And a few broad-gauged individuals assess the whole cosmos involved and develop the *strategy* that gives meaning and direction to it all—and determines whether anything meaningful will be accomplished.

In limited areas and with limited goals, carrying out specific activities without such an overall strategy can have its values. This may be the case where product publicity is desired to augment the other exposures of the product and its uses. It may be helpful to a politician or an entertainer who needs to become known to the public. To some extent, it is of value to a company whose stock is offered to the public or that needs to be known to prospective employees.

In most cases, however, the entire value of the mass communications operation will depend on the caliber and thoroughness of the analysis and thinking that precede the execution of techniques. This is as true for noncorporate organizations as it is for a big business.

Providing this caliber of intelligence calls for:

a. Breadth of scope capable of seeing the whole of the organization's "universe" together and understanding how the various elements affect each other.

b. Judgment capable of evaluating the significance of various symptoms, and of the soundness of suggestions for action or inaction in any given situation.

c. Diversity of experience and education, with as much training as possible in all the tactics and techniques of mass communication.

d. Creativity, both in bringing forth ideas and recommendations, and in expressing them so they will persuade others.

e. Objectivity—being far enough removed from intricacies of the organization to see it as others do, and forthright enough to express the viewpoint of these outsiders to the management.

This is a formidable combination of attributes. It is at this critical level, therefore, that the highest caliber of internal executive or counsel makes the great difference between various organizations' efforts in managing the human climate.

The vital planning process draws in thought, ideas, and information from every conceivable source, including especially those outside the organization itself.

It avoids any predetermined viewpoints that could block out innovative actions or changes in the approach.

It disdains formulas or patterns that have been set up for other programs; each situation is likely to be unique, and following others' patterns is a sure way to be at least partly wrong.

It tries to make sure that the organization is always adjusting to new trends, new problems, and new challenges. Today's organization must be dedicated to being in confluence with the course of the future—"with it" rather than bucking it.

Planning should make sure that the organization will be the

kind, and will have the kind of staff, that will be in tune with the *different* challenges sure to arise in the next 10 to 20 years, rather than trying to perpetuate patterns that have evolved out of a past that is obsolete.

In a period of rapid change in many areas, the old method of making one adjustment at a time, now and then, is sure to be behind the needs—especially in the ephemeral area of human attitudes.

chapter 50 Commanding the course of change in attitudes

Since change will inevitably happen to every organization, management has only two real courses in dealing with the human climate: (1) to let change overtake it and try to react; or (2) to take the initiative in helping to create the future climate in which it will have to function.

Many managers proceed on the basis that they should have command of the situation and thereby prevent what they do not approve.

For years, the men's and boys' clothing industry conducted their businesses as though the trend toward informal dress was an aberration and an affront to them, rather than a basic change in male attitude toward dress. The manufacturers not only resisted facing the consequences to their business plans but spent several million dollars running advertisements that tried to convince men that they were wrong and the manufacturers were right. The ads proclaimed: "Dress right! You can't afford not to."

The manufacturers of men's hats went through much the same

process: for years they tried to convince men that hatters knew better and that hats must be worn.

The motion picture industry reacted to television as an interloper and treated the public as if they were wayward children who should be lured back home.

Similarly, many managers face the inevitable changes in human attitudes that affect their organizations as if they are at best inconveniences and at worst misguided threats.

When they look at other businesses or organizations and at society as a whole, they recognize that change is rapid and multidimensional. Except for their own operations, they are aware that mere resistance to changing attitudes is likely to be futile, and that it is wise to read the trends and to try to have an influence on them.

Yet the majority of organizations still conduct their communications activities on a day-to-day or month-to-month basis and do little to create the climate of a couple of years hence. They pride themselves on long-range planning for financial needs, plant capacity, personnel requirements and training, materials needs, and other tangible matters for several years ahead. Yet the climate that will determine whether and how they use all of these is relegated to short-term consideration.

This is especially damaging in this era in which most organizations are under duress.

Living in someone else's climate

The organization or industry that waits until someone attacks it and then tries to overcome the attack is living in a climate being made by its opponents. It's breathing other people's air.

Almost all public relations and public affairs programs today are reacting to the initiative of opponents in an unfavorable climate of public attitudes.

The universities, the petroleum industry, banking, medicine, the media, consumer goods manufacturers, the securities industry, and many others are concentrating mostly on meeting present problems that might have been forestalled or alleviated if they had led their targets—if they had worked on creating the climate of public attitudes well before the attacks.

This condition is compounded by two common traits of today's managements:

1. There is extreme emphasis on immediate results as measured in the profit-and-loss statement or the organization report. This year—indeed, this quarter—is made to look as good as possible even when discretion calls for investment of some present resources in preparing for a better future.

2. The tangible aspects get the most attention, even in future investment, so when economy is considered to make the present look as good as possible, it is the intangible investments that are cut. Appropriations for plants and facilities needed through years in the future—usually large—are maintained while the modest budgets for building a favorable climate are usually the first to be cut and suffer the severest reductions.

Given the present pressures on managers for immediate favorable results, it is natural that these conditions should prevail. This situation requires that boards of directors, stockholders, or members assume a greater responsibility for encouraging the managers to maintain the long-term view in the crucial human-climate area.

To make the public resistant to the contagious disease of enemies' attacks, they have to be inoculated by facts and understanding well in advance. Inoculation is far less painful, far less expensive, and far more effective than coping with the virus after it has struck.

In the same way, a modest continuing expenditure for building a favorable climate is far better management judgment than waiting until severe problems strike and then spending heavily, with far less chance of success, to cope with them.

Commanding the course of attitudes calls for a thoroughly planned and executed program that inoculates against possible future attacks and builds acceptance that can accelerate many of the organization's objectives.

chapter 51 Essential factors in the program

THE planning process in a program to shape the human climate should incorporate a number of principles that will guide what is undertaken and how it is done:

1. *There must be a clear-cut conception of the organization's role and character*—so clearly defined it can readily be projected to outsiders in ways they will pay attention to.

2. *The organization's publics must be clearly understood.* They will differ—often bitterly opposing each other. Communications must be suited to reach each, knowing that often one or more groups will disagree sharply.

3. *The audiences have more subjects to concern them and less chance to understand them all.* They screen out more and more of what confronts them. Couching things in the self-interest of the audience is now mandatory.

4. *No organization now can afford to let the climate of attitudes develop by accident or through outside forces.* It must work to create its own climate.

5. *This calls for constant efforts to anticipate . . .* to read trends that may create the climate to be coped with.

6. *Time is a vital factor.* Careful contemplation is a luxury of

the past. Critics live in the real-time world of the TV camera and the dramatic event. A few minutes can be crucial, a day late is dead for sure.

7. *In a world of skepticism and activist critics, third-party supporters and spokesmen are more vital than ever.*

8. *The visible and the active must be stressed.* Even statements should be dramatized and made into events.

9. *Face-to-face interchange remains vital,* even in a mass-communication age (although there are limitations that often are unrecognized, as we shall see in Chapter 55).

a. It is the surest way to get a real feel for how the publics really think and how they respond to what you have to say.

b. It is demonstrable evidence of your real concern for them and their needs. You become humans they can start to understand and appreciate, rather than symbols of power who represent outsiders.

c. It is visible. Face-to-face contact is not the visibility of being on television in thousands of homes at once, but it is still visibility that represents reality to those you deal with.

10. *Even when people expose themselves to messages, they are moving targets, and only briefly.* Simplify . . . clarify . . . condense . . . illustrate.

11. *Stress mass-impact communications, reaching many people with each effort.* And stress pushing ideas and messages, not just servicing routine needs.

In addition, each organization needs to bring out how it is distinctive from others in its same category. One steel company is sued for high pollution levels . . . and all steel companies feel the public and government backlash. A couple of conglomerates show weak earnings and the chill sets in for most conglomerates. Some colleges suffer chaos because of anarchy on campus and most colleges suffer losses of support from alumni or legislatures.

People think in categories. They see the "youth problem," not the problems of millions of individual young people; Big Business, not hundreds of big businesses.

The problem is compounded by the massive number of identities people are confronted with and the growing complexity of organizations, which rubs out disparate traits of smaller, specialized entities.

This makes many organizations vulnerable to what happens to others in their "category." Bad practices or bad luck of a competitor or a "neighbor" in the same field may cause undue harm to their own acceptance.

This cannot be avoided entirely (making it vital to work for high standards throughout the field in which the organization functions). But anticipatory thinking and development of the organization's climate can soften the impact.

The keys to an organization's dealing with these problems are: (1) *distinctiveness;* (2) *visibility.*

1. *Select one or two features of the organization that characterize it and differentiate it from all others.* Be sure they are real differences and capable of being projected sharply.

2. *Select one or two means of projecting these differences.* It may be the character of the chief executive . . . a record of innovation . . . visible forms of acclaim.

Think ahead to the next transition in management so you won't lose all benefits of your efforts and have to start over.

3. *Use many channels for projection.* No single medium reaches a majority of the people today. "Opinion leaders" now seldom lead enough opinions. You must have a "multiple channel" communications program.

4. *Watch the feedback carefully.* Steer your course according to anticipation of the trends and a reading of your impact.

chapter 52 The importance of visibility

- President Nixon preempts television time to go directly to the people.
- Activists stage their protests to force media to focus on them.
- College students confront administrators, instead of writing editorials or signing petitions.
- Women's liberation leaders discard their bras and otherwise refuse to look as men want them to.

THIS is the "now" of present-day communications. The key is visibility.

Ideas and facts are still important, but it is how they are packaged to be seen that counts most.

Senators and cabinet members still make speeches. But it's the one before TV cameras at the Congressional hearing that makes the real impact.

Milton Friedman became a widely followed economist because he came to the visible attention of business and opinion leaders.

John Kenneth Galbraith uses a flair for self-publicity to become a much greater influence than many other respected scholars in his field.

What does this mean for business and other organizations? It will make a big difference in the fate of many organizations and perhaps of our way of life.

Here are a few clues:

1. *In conflicts between those who know how to use visibility and those who are sheltered, the sheltered will probably suffer.*

Student activists versus cloistered college presidents . . . dramatic consumerists versus methodical businessmen . . . visible environmentalists versus busy industrialists—regardless of opposing merits, the visible groups get the jump in public and government acceptance.

2. *More than ever, the anonymous institution, business, or industry will be at a disadvantage.*

This is compounded by the trend to sterile names, such as XYZ, Inc. An age of visibility—of TV and movies, of opinion being formed in the streets—is unsympathetic to the anonymous and the austere.

An institution has the advantage when it has a live, forceful spokesman with the ability to frame ideas so they depict concepts, such as Henry Ford II and S. I. Hayakawa, past-president of San Francisco State College. Anonymity and aloofness by leaders are increasingly costly.

3. *Methods used to communicate must change faster.*

Most organizations still do the bulk of their nonproduct communicating with methods dominant in the 19th century— speeches, printed matter, newspapers, magazines. Well over two thirds of people's input is now from visual media: audio-visuals, TV, movies, and face-to-face encounters.

Forces toward invisibility

A number of prominent trends in recent management practice militate against the effective visibility of organizations. Accordingly, while they tend to be gospel in the halls where professional management training is given, they represent threats to the survival of many managements. They include:

• The trends toward bigness and multidimension of organizations. The more complex the organization, the more difficult it is to convey a visible and understandable image of it. Each unit, to the extent that it is visible at all, conveys a somewhat different impression from the other units. The dynamics of managing the complex organization tend toward homogenization as a counteraction to splintering and organizational chaos.

• The trend toward executive isolation. As organizations become bigger and as the problems that managers must cope with multiply, they become immersed in their roles and have additional layers between them and the publics of concern to the organization.

• The trend toward incestuous internalization. Any organization that feels it is so big and so potent that it should have all of the skills within itself, cuts itself off from the wide horizons that can be brought in by intelligent outsiders as consultants and specialists. Members of the organization who deal almost entirely with each other tend to reflect each other and to reinforce each other's inclinations and prejudices.

• The trend toward bureaucratization of organizations, with even top executives considered to be parts of a team. This makes it prudent for executives to maintain a "low profile" and for no one to become indentifiable as a distinctive and visible personality.

• The trend toward treating the organization as the reality and the people in it as transient cogs. When it is expected that a man will become a chief executive at 54 and automatically retire at 65, his identity as a leader of the organization tends to be looked on, even by him, as a transitory stage in the immortality of the organization.

- The trend toward being propitiatory in dealing with all kinds of groups. It is considered bad form for many managers to be conspicuously identified with a viewpoint that may not be favored by all aspects of all groups that are of concern to the organization. Carried to an extreme, this makes ideological eunuchs of many managers.
- The inherent instinct of the manager for confidentiality that motivates him to keep his activities and information to himself. Knowledge of what he knows or does, in the hands of those now on his team, is seen as a threat to his autonomy in making decisions. His natural sense of competitiveness causes him to balk at the possibility of providing competitors—or others who can make inroads into his territory—with anything they might find useful.

As in many other aspects of today's complexities of management, there are direct conflicts between some of the factors involved.

While it is true that all of these trends seem to make it prudent for the manager to be anonymous and for the organization to maintain its low profile, it is also true that doing so is contributing to the mounting threats to the survival of many organizations.

chapter **53** **The end of anonymity**

THE proliferation of activist dissenters and the growth of criticism of all organizations by the media are combining to change the rules under which established institutions have functioned.

Many of the organizations of critics have demonstrated a shrewd knowledge of how to use the media. At the same time, many of the media—faced with growing competition for the attention and the acceptance of the audience—are turning to the role of crusader to command attention.

This combination of the critics' knowledge of how to use the media and the receptivity to them of many of the media turns the spotlight on what previously were protected corners.

As we have seen, the new activist-media force is the "smart bomb" of our modern social system. It is able to seek out what were previously low-profile organizations and institutions and attack them. Hundreds of groups and firms that "minded their own business" for years have found themselves blasted in their once-impregnable bunkers.

Some of the most comfortable havens have felt the blasts: universities, foundations, churches, and even the media. Companies and industries that had kept their roles quietly behind the scenes are among the most attacked today.

In fact, there seems to be a direct correlation between the recessive posture of an organization and its vulnerability to attacks when they come. The universities and foundations, for instance, assumed for many years that it was unseemly for them to be "aggressive" in seeking public recognition. Their leadership not only was disinclined toward actively publicizing and promoting their interests but untrained in the necessary orientation and techniques.

Here are a few guidelines for managers who must now consider that they are open to harsh scrutiny and attack, regardless of other circumstances:

1. *Companies, institutions, industries, and individuals are all "in bounds" to the activist critics.* The right to privacy is being eroded for individuals, but it is being blasted away for organizations. Few functions will retain confidentiality.

2. *Impersonal organizations and industries are most vulnerable to attack because their size is visible and they seem like inhuman monoliths instead of human institutions.* The cloak of anonymity of much of business (a handful of business leaders are known to the public today) should be replaced with personalization, visibility, and humanization.

3. *A "low profile" indicates secretiveness.* At a time when millions of people feel entitled to have a say about how all institutions function and when all organizations are under suspicion, the impression of being secretive automatically creates distrust. It inevitably is pounced upon as evidence that the organization has something to hide. Lyndon Johnson's big credibility gap was due as much to his trying to keep things from the people as to falsification.

4. *The new educated populace tends to take no truths to be self-evident.* It is necessary to expose an organization's rationale,

purpose, and functions to the cold-eyed evaluation of the public, and to use the deftest and most skilled communications to gain acceptance.

For generations, the goal of many organizations was to build themselves an entrenched position and to operate behind its closed doors, presenting to the public only the facade they wished to project. Today, entrenchment with a low profile tends to make an organization a sitting duck to the "smart bomb" activist-media complex.

The best defense is an open posture and defusing the critical "bombs" through visible actions and effective communications.

chapter 54 Selecting the messages

THE converse of the error of doing too little to cope with the human climate is trying to do too much. A few key messages can be projected; a lot of miscellaneous ones cannot.

Each division of an organization, such as a product category or subsidiary of a corporation, may have its own communications program. But these must have a consistency and unity for the organization as a whole. There should be a core of concepts and guidelines for all elements of the organization.

There are no hermitically sealed cells within an organization's reputation. What affects one element affects all.

a. What happens to a company's employees affects the attitude of stockholders, the community, and the government.

b. What happens to it in Germany affects its operations in Chile.

c. How it is regarded by its employees affects its chances of getting the best future employees on which its own future depends.

The reputation of any organization is indivisible. In addition, it is wise for each organization to convey clearly its purpose and the reason for expecting the public's acceptance. To do this, it should relate its purpose to the self-interest of the audiences, however disparate they may be.

The managements of business organizations want to talk about the blessings that free enterprise has created; the earners of salaries and wages want to hear who will fulfill their multiple expectations.

The motivations of various groups seem to be not only opposite but in opposition. Yet they have in common the fact that they are motivations—that almost everyone in our society has his incentive.

Incentives vary as widely as the aspirations and lifestyles that now make up American society. Each group is motivated by incentives that are meaningful to them, but each group fails to understand why other people do things—and that underlies much of the failure of communication.

The incentives that motivate business, for instance, are peculiarly its own. They are not the same as the incentives of academicians, writers, and devotees of communal living; so these groups fail to understand that business' incentives are vital to their own feeding, housing, clothing, transportation, and lighting.

Accordingly, every organization should have, as one of its basic messages, the concept of how its efforts to achieve its goals serve the interests of others who, though they have other and even conflicting goals, derive important benefits.

Part of this is projecting clearly what is distinctive and useful about the organization.

No two organizations are alike. The organization's unique character should be stressed, as well as its role in meeting a general function.

And how the organization plans and carries out its functions as a responsible entity should be sharply defined in its communications. Those who live within an organization, like the members of a family, come to take its role and character for granted, but the public doesn't.

The variety of approaches to carrying out this function is great, because of the great diversity of organizations. It is therefore especially important that anything resembling a formula be avoided. In this area, broad experience and professional judgment that have been developed through dealing with a wide variety of organizational situations are invaluable.

chapter 55   Selecting and reaching the audiences

Unity and consistency of the communication from an organization should be combined with the growing need to pinpoint messages to each audience.

The segmented populace and the growing individuality of people lessen the chance that one treatment will motivate all groups. In fact, in many cases what will appeal to one segment is certain to repel another.

The total thrust and content of the communication must be consistent, but the messages should be directed in the context of each group, whenever possible. Therefore, careful attention is needed in defining all the organization's audiences and then keeping them clearly in mind when each phase of the program is conducted.

Each organization will have differences in the makeup of its publics, but the basic ones are likely to be:

1. Personnel.
2. Stockholders or members.
3. Governments.
4. Customers (and perhaps dealers).
5. The community, including minority groups

    6. Special-interest groups—consumerist organizations, ecology societies, youth groups.

Now it is time to throw the light of caution onto what has become a cliche of our times: that the answer to misunderstandings between diverse and opposing groups is "involvement"— which usually is taken to mean overcoming differences through frank and open interchange.

For years it has been a widely held tenet that friction between groups of people is the result of separateness; that if only they could be brought together and "get to know each other" they would develop mutual respect and understanding.

That is the principle behind "involvement" and "sitting down together," both of which have many vocal adherents.

But like many "rules," it is often untrue. Few groups are more "involved" with each other or understand each other so well as the Protestants and Catholics in Northern Ireland, the Turks and Greeks on Cyprus, the French and English descendants in Quebec, the East and West Pakistanis, neighboring tribes in Nigeria, the Jews and Arabs in the Middle East, the North and South Vietnamese, the blacks and whites in Rhodesia . . . and millions of husbands and wives everywhere.

Close involvement often *emphasizes* differences more than similarities.

So not only is the faith in "education" as a cure for all human problems likely to be unfounded but so is "interchange."

For managers this means:

1. Consider interchange and involvement with all publics. Often they can lead to improved relations. But *assess realistically* what the varied viewpoints are.

Which are areas where mutual interests may be furthered, and where might relationships only be rubbed raw?

2. Don't let the fabled optimism of America's orientation to selling color judgment on group relationships.

The confident salesman feels he can sell anyone whatever he wants to sell. The reality of group dynamics argues against that possibility where groups have wide differences.

Involvement is a form of interchange with both high potential value and some serious risks. Judge the chances for progress soberly and realistically. Lyndon Johnson's faith in "reasoning together" never reconciled the antiwar groups.

3. Determine your course on the basis of what's sound for your organization, your stockholders or members, society as a whole —and then, if feasible, for other groups that have different goals.

chapter 56   The seven factors of persuasion

There are seven factors that are integral to the process of convincing and motivating an audience. Now we can view them as they apply to carrying out a sound program in managing the human climate:

1. *Acceptability.*

Unless the source of information is respected and objective, communication is less likely to take place. The statement or claim should reach the person when he is preset to acceptance—when he has opened his mind to a spokesman he is willing to have invade the privacy of his inner convictions. An unknown or suspected spokesman can cause him to close his mind and even to resent the person who makes the effort to change his thinking.

2. *Compatibility.*

The message must relate to the recipient's posture of thought and identity. People reject or distort whatever is alien to their heritage, background, and sources of self-assurance. They respond to what reinforces their conception of themselves and their view of the world.

3. *Intensity.*

The degree of impact of the message is determined by the prominence it receives in competition with many other efforts to capture the attention. Information presented casually or in a mass of other information has much less impact than information presented prominently and in isolation.

4. *Visibility.*

The communication that is most nearly real, that involves the person by making him almost a part of it, has the greatest power to sway him. In early days, it was the drama and the "revivalist" platform artist that were most activating; today, it is television and the film.

5. *Pervasiveness.*

When a subject appears to be all around him, a person tends to accept it and take it for granted. It becomes part of the atmosphere in which he lives. He finds himself surrounded by it and absorbs the climate of the idea.

6. *A variety of impressions.*

Pervasiveness results from encountering a subject in a wide variety of ways. As we have seen, this multiple-channel approach to persuasion is vital.

7. *Persuasiveness.*

No amount of impact, variety, or pervasiveness will influence attitudes and opinions unless the context of the communications is persuasive. It must be most deftly developed to reach into the subconscious of the person and tune to his urges, interests, and desires. Mere expression of the communicator's point of view will not succeed; it must be attuned to the mental and emotional bent of the audience.

chapter 57 How to affect opinion

By relating your message to one or more of the following entrées to the individual's psyche, the message can become a part of his psychological make-up:[1]

1. *Reporting changes in the relevant environment.*

When the individual can clearly see that a change has taken place that he must acknowledge, he can rationalize a change in viewpoint. Perhaps the most striking example is the present attitude of Americans toward the Japanese and German peoples, both of which had been the objects of hatred during World War II.

2. *Enhancing existing patterns of behavior.*

Determining what information people want and then providing it can gain their support for related information or viewpoints.

3. *Selectively reinforcing existing attitudes.*

People often want conflicting things, such as both better schools and lower taxes. By selectively focusing on the strong points of one of these, the communicator may enable the person to settle on that one even though he must give up the desirability of the other one.

4. *Focusing attention.*

For instance, there often are many issues in an election campaign that are of some interest to various voters. A candidate who focuses on one issue to the point of making those voters strongly aware of their self-interest in it is able to get their vote even though he may not conform to the voters' viewpoint on the other issues.

5. *Activating existing attitudes.*

A person may be a silently loyal alumnus of his college but do nothing to help it. If communications bring his loyalty to the active stage, he may be persuaded to contribute funds or to recommend the school to the prize high school students in his area.

6. *Developing new interests and attitudes.*

A person may have never thought of participating in skiing. Yet he may see a thrilling and beautiful motion picture of skiing in the Swiss Alps and be motivated to take up the sport.

7. *Suggesting new patterns of behavior.*

When confronted with a major change in condition, an individual develops a strong receptivity to information that will help him. For example, someone who has never thought about living in Kansas City becomes very receptive to information that will help him when he is about to be transferred, and will be amenable to the viewpoint of the organization that provides that information.

Communication intended to influence other people is one of the oldest of human practices, yet it is still one of the least known. These principles are distilled from the limited amount of research that has been meaningful in this field and from years of successful observation and application of mass-audience communications for a wide range of successful organizations.

It can be seen from this list that a casual, "natural" approach to changing or forming group attitudes is as unlikely to be really successful as a similar approach to winning the Olympic pole vault or the world chess championship. This is a complex and intricate science as well as a practice with many nuances and techniques. It requires substantial talent that is honed by extensive training. It is not surprising, therefore, that it is said by authoritative observers of mass communication that the ineffective programs greatly outnumber those that achieve a degree of success.

From the principles and components of a successful program we can now move to an examination of techniques.

chapter 58   The techniques to use

Today's professionally trained manager knows that he cannot be expert in most of the areas where his responsibility will be called on. He learns to depend on experts in science, law, production, taxes, and other fields, while exerting his judgment in using their expertness.

Unfortunately, this leaves many managers with the urge to retain operating control in areas where they think the complexities are not great. Dealing with the techniques of mass communication is one of the areas that most often looks attractive to the manager. These techniques look, on the surface, like "just common sense" and deal with things he feels familiar with. After all, didn't he learn to write and speak, and doesn't he watch television, listen to radio, read newspapers and magazines, and listen to people?

Also, all professionals in mass communication assert constantly that no program can be really effective unless there is active participation by top management executives.

However, *participation* should not be defined as *operation*. The nuances and skills in this field are even more difficult for most managers to master themselves than the technical areas—which, after all, are tangible and thus in keeping with their training.

So it is important that the manager understand the importance of the human climate to every aspect of his operation, but that he call on the judgment and abilities of the best available professionals.

There are seven basic techniques that the manager should be aware of. Program recommendations he may consider can include most or all of these. A good program is likely to include a balance of a number of them.

1. *Actions and visible events.*

The massive demands on people's attention make it difficult for any message to break through to them. The emergence of television and films has helped make this an age of visibility. Communication by words alone is becoming less and less able to reach and motivate audiences.

For more than two years in his first term, President Nixon—as well as Agnew, Mitchell, Laird, *et al*—commandeered the media for statements and rhetoric. The popularity of the administration went down. Then Nixon pushed withdrawal from Vietnam, announced new relations with Red China, put forth Phase I economic controls and the import surcharge, bearded George Meany in the AFL-CIO den, and brought forth an international monetary settlement. The popularity of the administration shot up. With the mounting revelations of the Watergate affair and other machinations of his re-election and headquarters staffs, his popularity plunged again.

There couldn't be a clearer demonstration: this is an age of visible action, not just words.

What an organization does and shows about the issues on its publics' minds makes what it says credible—in advertisements, speeches, press releases, and everything else.

2. *Involvement.*

An organization and executives who are isolated from their publics lose visibility and credibility.

In spite of the growth of mass communications media, the importance of face-to-face interchange has increased. Managers must be seen and heard on matters of concern to their publics. Organizations must be seen to take a serious role in the dynamics of the groups they deal with. There must be a fine line between domination, that is viewed as paternalism, and isolation, which is viewed as arrogant neglect. And, as we have seen, it is important to view realistically what can be attained by involvement.

3. *Publicity.*

Though dissemination of information is not to be regarded as the focal point of a human-climate program, it is a vital function that makes other elements effective.

For most organizations, all of the following elements will be important in a sound publicity effort. However, while the manager is likely at some time to be involved with all of them, it is only in the last of these (speeches) that he will be wise to assume the execution himself. Each of these media of communication has many elements to be known and judged and must be pursued by an experienced and skilled professional.

Accordingly, while the manager might well benefit from an acquaintance with the basics of these techniques (such as appear in my *Lesly's Public Relations Handbook*, pages 329–482) that knowledge should be applied in the same way as is knowledge about computers or injection molding—as a basis for judgment and evaluation, rather than for self-utilization.

It is important to recognize that what is germane in each of these media areas will vary greatly among organizations, depending on the locations of their operations, the nature of their functions, the history of their previous publicity efforts, the nature of what they have to report, and other factors.

The Media to Use

The media that would be considered in almost all publicity programs include:

- Newspapers—metropolitan and community
- Press services and syndicates
- General magazines
- Specialized magazines—business, farm, religious, labor, minority, hobby, etc.
- Free-lance writers
- Television
- Radio
- Trade or professional publications
- Newsletters
- Letters (aside from individualized correspondence)
- Posters, displays, and exhibits
- Printed literature
- Motion pictures and slidefilms

It is also important to monitor the results of publicity efforts to provide guides to future efforts. And there are advantageous ways to merchandise the results that appear in the form of clippings, broadcast reports, photographic records, filmed footage, reports to employees and stockholders, distribution to dealers, and so on.

4. *Relations with media personnel.*

5. *House publications.*

6. *Promotions and other events*—anniversaries, rallies, recognition ceremonies, etc.

7. *Speeches.*

Few speeches should have as their prime purpose the audience to which they are actually delivered. The 50 to 1,500 in attendance may be important, but usually there's a bigger audience to be reached beyond the meeting room.

Unusual skill is required to produce a speech eminently effective with the audience, but also effective with the thousands who will hear or read it elsewhere. Many organizations consider a job done when the speech is delivered and printed copies are mailed out (at an average cost of around 20¢). But those are the immediately available means, and not the most effective potentially.

Here are some tips on getting full effectiveness from a speech:

a. Each speech (except a technical presentation) should be approached with the question: How wide an audience can be reached through all media—TV, newspapers, magazines, radio, trade press? Account for the possibilities in that order: TV is least likely but possible under good conditions, for instance.

b. Make it quotable. Important points, pithy phrases, new thoughts, provocative issues can catch an editor's interest. A large percentage of speeches, even when having something worthwhile to say, stifle efforts to pick out the quotes that will make a story. How a speech is written ranks with its substance. If it's good copy, it's likely to be good listening too.

c. Make sure the substance is there. Few statements can capture attention if they restate common theses—the need for cooperation, the dangers of unrestrained criticism, this is an era of change and adjustment, and so on. If a speech has nothing important to say that's new, why should it be given at all?

d. Be sure it's timely. The old verities make good sermons but poor speeches. If the substance fits today's headlines and adds a dimension or two, it's on the track.

e. Help the media judge it. Few things are as forbidding to editors as multipage speech manuscripts. Mark the important and the quotable passages boldly. Include a covering press release treating the highlights or a memo of explanation. Get it to the media several days early, with a release date.

A good speech, well prepared and well handled, is worth 50 ordinary platform appearances.

It is vital that the professionals keep the manager abreast of the rapid changes occurring in mass communications.

The lag in methods used—already a severe handicap to responsible organizations—will grow worse unless they are ready to make good use of the new techniques as they develop. Already great strides are being made by some organizations in using cable television, sound and video cassettes, closed-circuit television, and packaged learning materials.

Publicity activities should not be carried out without a thorough analysis of the organization and its place in the currents that make up the human climate. Executing the techniques of publicity without such a thoughtful understanding is at best wasteful and at worst as harmful as operating an airline without continuous weather reports.

SECTION VII Administering the program

chapter 59 Staffing the human-climate program

MANY managers are becoming increasingly con-
fused about the entire field of mass-communications services. Just
when the term "public relations" was beginning to gain fairly
broad understanding, there has arisen a wide range of euphemisms and new terms that seek to replace it.

The term "public relations" has become the victim of a number of trends and conditions:

• The vocal left has attacked it as the symbol of the establishment
they hate. Since they feel that none of the organizations in that
establishment can be defensible, the function that proposes to
defend and to gain support for an organization is considered
abominable. Through the liberal-leaning media and other efforts, they have increasingly associated the "public relations"
identification with the alleged sinfulness of all established organizations.

• By act of Congress in 1913 all federal government offices have
been forbidden to use the term "public relations." All members
of Congress use its principles and practices in each election, but
they look at it askance in government. Appropriations for that

function are illegal. Accordingly, federal and military offices have become practiced in using euphemisms, such as Public Information Office, Public Affairs Office, Assistant to the Secretary, and the like.

• The antiorganization forces have joined with others in propounding the concept that public relations is entirely a cover-up process, rather than a constructive function in helping an organization come into confluence with its publics. Media and public officials alike have frequently been quoted to the effect that every effort to put a good face on things is a "public relations gimmick."

• Many people—including many within the field itself—have persisted in using the term "public relations" when only "publicity" is meant. This is equivalent to talking about medicine as a profession when only the prescription of specific medicines is involved, but it has had widespread exposure.

• Additionally, lurid novels and movies, as well as some of the most conspicuous members of the craft, have conveyed the impression that public relations is essentially a glad-handing and party-giving function.

As a result, two things have been happening to the terminology in the field:

1. Public relations people themselves, and often the organizations they work for, have been turning to other terms. Often these compound the problem rather than solve it. In many cases they focus on one aspect of the total, much as publicity people have focused on one aspect in the past. Thus terms such as "public affairs," "corporate affairs," "communications," "external affairs," and others treat a part of the total spectrum as if it were the whole.

2. As managers have felt the need for expertness and help in new problem areas of the human climate, such as minority rela-

tions or government relations, they have not looked to those public relations practitioners who are well qualified in these areas because the managers have not recognized those skills as belonging to public relations people. Instead, they have often sought out former government officials, specialized lawyers, members of minority groups, and others and given them "public affairs," "government relations," or other titles.

The term "managing the human climate" may be seen as adding a dimension to all others by putting increased emphasis on helping to create the climate of attitudes that the organization will encounter in the future.

This matter of terminology should be put into perspective because it is important to a manager in considering how to obtain the services required to meet needs in this field. It is not the terminology used but the definition of the functions and the caliber of the people involved that count.

It is too early to predict how the definitions of the field will sift down. It is likely that if the functions continue to be essentially what public relations in the true sense has covered, any new titles will soon develop the same associations in people's minds as public relations has done.

The functions of staff

Aside from terminology, the staffing and operation of the human-climate program should be based on the functions to be performed.

While staffing in practice will often involve both internal personnel and external counsel and services, in this chapter we will focus on the internal staff and its functions.

The basic functions are:

1. *Advice.*

The human-climate staff should work with the top management of the organization and with its divisions, subsidiaries, or affiliates. It is the sensory organ responsible for judging what the actions, policies, and statements of the organization are likely to do to the publics they affect and for judging what the attitudes and trends of the publics may imply for the management.

Thus it may be visualized as the switchboard in the system of interrelationships between the people in the organization and all the people both inside and outside with which the organization is concerned. They are the routing point that detects and directs the signals coming in from all directions and going out to almost all recipients.

The primary areas in which advice is involved include:

- Looking for and identifying trends and patterns of all aspects of society that may have a bearing on the operations and decisions of the organization. This, in effect, is the "early warning" function of sensing where ideas and movements may be going that the organization should be alerted to.
- Developing recommendations, programs, and communications activities for submission to management that will meet either current requirements or anticipated needs.
- Advising management in periods of emergency on how to respond, what actions to take, what statements to make, how to deal with the press, and related matters. Emergencies are of many types, from an explosion at a company plant to efforts by a militant organization to disrupt the meeting of a professional association.
- Reviewing and applying communications judgment to programs, policies, and statements under consideration by the management, before they are completed.

2. *Creative input.*

This involves submitting ideas bearing in any way on group attitudes within or outside the company; offering suggestions on matters under consideration within the organization; reviewing and revising communications materials from top management or any division requesting such advice; and providing liaison between elements of the organization and expert outsiders who have various expertness and skills.

3. *Participation in planning.*

As experienced specialists in mass responses and communications, the human-climate personnel are often able to provide an added dimension to the considerations of many elements of the organization.

Discussions of a proposed new line of products, for instance, can benefit from the input of such qualified people during the consideration stage—long before the development of specific communications about that product line are to be undertaken.

Similarly, considerations of plant locations, employment practices, campus recruitment, and many other functions can be benefited.

4. *Conducting communications functions.*

These tend to be of three types:

- Passive—issuing announcements, providing news reports, issuing periodicals, preparing annual reports and other regular documents, and so on.
- Service—dealing with the media, meeting internal communications needs such as working with managers in preparation of speeches and statements, reviewing written materials for top management or divisions, and so on.
- Initiative functions—stimulating the interests of media in the functions and messages of the organization, preparing recommendations to executives within the organization for new operations or changes in present ones, and so on.

The needs to be met

In any qualified human-climate operation, there is a composite of needs that should be met—as fully as possible—by the total staff and outside counsel or specialists, as needed. As many as possible of these qualifications should be embodied in the top human-climate executive. When that is not attainable, the composite should include as many of the traits as can be provided by a counsel who will be able to devote considerable time to that organization, plus its internal executive (see Chapter 61).

The needs are:

a. Experience. Few managers would feel comfortable about having their open-heart surgery performed by a neophyte. The complexities of the human-climate problems—as detailed throughout this book—call for a range of knowledge and skills that is attainable only through extensive study and broad practice.

b. Judgment. While this is sometimes a product of broad and deep experience, it is elusive even for many who have functioned in the field for years. The judgment required must be at the highest plane, of the type that commands respect and the acceptance of demanding executives throughout the organization and the groups it deals with.

c. Ability to work at the level of top management. Acceptance of human-climate or public-relations advisors by managers can come only out of respect for their experience, skills, judgment, and bearing. They need to be as confident of their competence in their area as the top manager is in his.

d. Sensitivity to the human factors. This would seem to be self-evident, yet many organizations promote a man to the top human-climate responsibility who has a background bereft of this sensitivity to the intangibles. Some lawyers, production people, and financial experts can make this transition, but some cannot.

e. Communication skills. The ability to conceptualize ideas, to frame means of communicating them, and to express them effectively is an indispensable requirement.

In some fields the top executives need not be skilled in the functions involved, but that is not true in mass communications.

The department manager will have difficulty judging what is needed, evaluating the work of his staff, offering suggestions to management, or performing effectively in most other areas unless he has both the gift and the training that make up exceptional communications ability.

f. Knowledge of all publicity media. Here the manager need not be fully versed on every nuance of how each newspaper, press service, magazine, TV outlet, and so on performs. But he must have a basic awareness of all of these fields, their needs, their means of operation, and their taboos.

g. Knowledge of all other communications techniques. Aside from the outside media mentioned, there are others that can be called "controlled media" because they originate with the organization and are completely developed by it. These include printed materials, periodicals, films, meetings, exhibits, and the like.

h. Speed. While the qualified and professional human-climate operation will seldom resemble the movie version of a newsroom, there are many occasions when time is critical. When the unexpected occurs and demands a reaction or response; when a review of a speech or a statement is required just before it is to be delivered; when an opinion is needed on a delicate situation immediately impending—in these and other situations, the ability to think and perform instantly is important.

i. High output. Again, the frenetic pace of the newsroom is seldom called for, but the slow, comtemplative output of the Ph.D. candidate working on his thesis is equally unsuitable. There is a great variation in the output between various human-climate or public-relations operations. Many that consider themselves productive are only modestly so when compared with really efficient and productive staffs.

j. Ability to work well "in the middle." Professionals in this area are constantly "men in the middle." They are the pivots between the organization and the media, the organization and other organizations, the organization and all types of people, and one department and another. They must be able to retain the confidence and respect of each side while dealing with their opposing concerns.

k. "Old-fashioned" virtues.   It is unfashionable—particularly among many "free-wheeling" people in the communication fields—to speak of these, but they are vital. The absence of any of them may well render useless a high degree of excellence in all the others. These virtues are loyalty, integrity, conscientiousness, and—since people in this field must always be basically unobtrusive—a readiness to work hard with or without special recognition.

chapter 60 Selecting staff

Because this field has developed rapidly, without the sort of identifiable training pattern that marks accounting, law, and many other disciplines, there is a temptation for managers to appoint people for the function because they are available, they know the organization, or they seem to be blessed with the right kind of personality.

Precisely because the requirements are so poorly defined, it is especially important that the search for personnel—especially the top executives—be conducted with the aid of widely experienced and discerning professionals. Even many of the most successful executive recruiters acknowledge their discomfort with most assignments to find qualified public-relations executives.

The field is narrow. While there are said to be 50,000 practitioners employed in it, that figure includes a wide range of limited and special skills, regional orientation, and other limitations. Knowing where the few qualified candidates may be, how to evaluate them, and how to interest them in making a move is a special talent.

Of course, qualified personnel executives and managers who have had experience in working with people in this field can evaluate and select men or women with a good degree of success. The important thing is to resist the temptation to fill the position with people who have outgrown their spots in some other discipline.

Screening of candidates is another area that calls for special care, especially in observing personality traits and habits.

One of the common psychological disabilities might be called "educated ineptitude." Some people with great talent and excellent training are stymied when faced with the requirements of constantly getting a job done and doing it well. Some are excellent at organizing their thoughts and sorting out what needs to be done but get bogged down along the route toward completing it. Others have a short span of enthusiasm and tend to peter out part way through.

Accordingly, in screening personnel in these fields, stress should be put on spotting the applicant's other IQ—his Ineptitude Quotient. Some of the questions to be explored include:

- Does he plan and organize before wanting to take off?
- Does he take each project through every step to conclusion and evaluation?
- Is he as interested in a project near the end as he was at the beginning?
- Does he do the boring essentials—checking over his work, keeping others posted—as readily as he does the "glamorous" things?
- Is he interested in the total mosaic of the operation and want to see it all succeed—including what he personally may not be involved in?
- Can he accept the reality that many efforts will show no success, and that many successes will derive no praise or will even be scuttled by politics?
- What increases when he encounters frustrations—his efforts to find new paths, or his smoking and drinking?

Men, women, and minority members

As part of the "equal opportunity" movement, there are overt efforts in many organizations to fill positions with women, blacks, or others. That policy has considerable merit where the nature of the function can accommodate people who need or are worthy of special consideration.

The public relations field has had a significant proportion of women for the past 25 years. It is true that in many instances women executives were primarily assigned to "women's interest" areas, such as product publicity on food, clothing, baby products, and the like. But in a number of instances, women executives have had broad general responsibilities.

There are a number of effective blacks in the field, including several who operate specialized counseling firms.

Because of the demanding requirements of the field and the seriousness of errors or inadequate judgment, it can justifiably be said that capability and the proper traits for the position involved should be the only criteria for selection. This will mean, of course, that many of the women employed will be primarily responsible for "women's interest" matters at the start and that many of the minority employees will at first deal primarily with minority relations matters. However, such starting points have been the launching pads for the great majority of top executives in the field; and the opportunity for a woman, a black, or anyone else to grow beyond the limitations of the starting specialty can be excellent.

Salaries and benefits

For a number of years, the remuneration has been comparatively high among the lower echelons in this field and comparable to other professional executives in the higher echelons.

The reason for this is essentially supply and demand. While there are a substantial number of inexperienced young people striving to enter the field, its rapid growth has meant there has always been a shortage of proved people with a few years of good experience. Then as people level off in their development, they level off at a somewhat-higher-than-standard salary level.

The recent burst of concern among managers for the human-climate problem has created a severe shortage of fully rounded, fully capable executives in the field.

There are no standard remuneration levels that can be charted and compared, as there are in many other fields. Also, salary levels will vary substantially among types of organization, such as the lower salaries paid by hospitals and colleges and the higher salaries paid by large corporations.

Surveys by the authoritative *PR Reporter* provide the most indicative clues to remuneration levels. The 1972 survey showed that the median salary for Directors of Public Relations (or equivalent titles) in companies with sales of less than $100 million was $20,000; in companies with sales of $100–$300 million it was $25,000; in companies of $300–$500 million it was $27,000; in companies of $500–$700 million it was $31,000; in companies of $700 million to $1 billion it was $31,000; and in companies of more than $1 billion it was $32,000. There are a number of vice presidents with this function, however, who receive more than $60,000 plus substantial benefits, with some above the $100,000 level.

Basis of operation

The operation of the human-climate staff will resemble in most respects that of other professional services. A few guidelines that are especially pertinent for this field are:

• Productivity and the freedom to function within the limits of the organization's basic policy should be encouraged. Rigidity stifles the most essential traits—innovativeness, creativity, initiative.

- The responsible executives should be treated with absolute candor and confidence. As has been pointed out, integrity is an indispensable trait, and the management must have full confidence in the people.

- The responsible executives should be involved at all times in the considerations and the functions they may have to deal with. A major proportion of their potential effectiveness is lost if they are not a party to the evolving considerations.

- Protection should be provided from the political machinations that exist in all organizations and that often entrap the communications personnel. No one department should be able to commandeer an undue proportion of their attention. Efforts to place the blame on them for unfavorable press reports or other circumstantial circumstances should be met with considerable skepticism.

chapter 61 Selection and use of counsel

Just as there is confusion caused by the many differing definitions of what public relations is, there is confusion about what functions are performed by the firms in the field.

The majority of "public relations counseling" firms—or those that use other descriptions—devote most of their efforts to getting publicity for their clients. This often includes nonmedia publicity, such as preparing literature or arranging meetings.

Other firms add to the publicity functions one or more specialties such as stockholder and investment-community relations.

Together, the all-publicity and the publicity-plus-special-services organizations represent perhaps 90 percent of the activity carried out by the firms in this field.

A few firms are qualified through at least one of their principals to provide mature and professional counsel in the areas that are covered in this book. Some of these also provide some or all of the service activities in publicity and the specialized fields. When they do, much of the time of their principals is devoted to these services or to managing the organization so it can provide the services.

A few firms concentrate on providing the skills and talents of their principals almost exclusively in the counseling and creative-input areas. They afford judgment and the benefit of experience in considerations that have public ramifications; make analyses; write major documents; guide internal staff; recruit and evaluate communications personnel; and, occasionally, perform specific publicity and specialized functions when they are desired.

There are further distinctions among the types of firm available to management. They can be characterized into five general categories:

1. The counseling and creative-input firm as described above.

2. The large "supermarket" organization that seeks, through the combined talents of a large staff, to be qualified in all the functional areas of human-climate services, including counseling.

3. The smaller but diversified jack-of-all-trades firm that takes on virtually any client who is willing to retain it. It may have a few large clients, but in general tends to have a clientele of medium-sized and smaller organizations. Accordingly, its principals may not have the broad and deep experience to qualify them as true counselors beyond the service areas that they function in.

4. Specialist firms in such fields as financial public relations, minority relations, government relations, public affairs, employee communications, and the like. Within their area of expertness, these firms provide counsel as well as services based on the range of their experience.

5. Firms that are essentially regional or local. There is considerable diversity among them, but their clientele and the scope of their operations are generally limited to the area in which their office is located. Their clients are likely to be local or regional retailers, hospitals, public-service organizations, smaller manufacturing companies, and so on.

There are reputable and highly competent firms in each of these categories. However, it is just as important for a manager to select a counseling firm that meets his profile of requirements as it is to select the right law firm for each type of requirement.

Benefits provided

There are basically three purposes that an outside firm can provide:

1. Wide experience, extensive and sound judgment, creativity, and a high degree of skills.

2. Objectivity—bringing seasoned consideration based on an outside viewpoint into the otherwise ingrown thinking precesses of the organization's own management and staff. Because the human-climate factors are intangible and largely immeasurable, there is hardly any way to sense when inbred thinking is deluding everyone unless such an objective input and checking process is included.

Physicians see other physicians when they have a health problem, and lawyers bring in other lawyers when they have a need outside their specialty.

Contrary to widespread opinion, the need for this kind of objective thinking is greatest among the biggest and most complex organizations. The very sense of omnipotence that size and power tend to create among an organization's executives provides a fertile culture for shutting out the freshness of thought and the probing questions that are vital. An outstanding example of how deluded an executive can be when he is limited to inside advice was President Nixon in connection with the Watergate affair.

3. Augmenting the internal staff. The firm dovetails its resources with those of the organization's personnel by filling in gaps in talents (such as speech writing and financial reporting), geographic locations (such as media-relations personnel in New York, Chicago, or Washington) and carrying out specific functions such as an anniversary program, the introduction of a new

product, and other activities for which an internal staff will not be permanently employed.

4. Knowledge of the communications media and acquaintance with media staff people. An organization that works for a number of clients is likely to have current experience with a wide range of media. Because it contacts media people on a variety of subjects, it is likely to be dealing with them more frequently than persons working for a single organization.

Basis of operation

There are essentially three forms of arrangement for utilizing the outside firm:

1. The counsel is called on by both the top management and the internal staff executive. Where dealings are held with top management, they generally then will be executed through joint planning and allocation between the internal staff and the counseling firm.

2. The firm will deal primarily with the Director of Public Relations (with whatever title), dealing with other management executives as needed or requested. Even though one of the purposes of the firm may be counseling and creative input, this arrangement tends to make the firm essentially an adjunct to the internal department.

3. The firm is assigned specific functions and reports to the Director of Public Relations or his equivalent. These may include continuing program activities, such as product publicity or financial communications.

When the management executive is concerned primarily with paragraph 1 above, the following working pattern between the management and the counsel is recommended.

This plan should include:

1. Determining the scope of decision-making and policy-discussing processes of the organization in which the counsel should

be included. The right counsel can make positive contributions to many kinds of policy considerations and to creative planning, as well as provide recommendations on the mass communications functions involved. So getting his input at the strategy-forming level can be one of the greatest values to be derived from the relationship.

If it is decided not to have the counsel participate in these, it is wise to fill him in on the considerations of these groups by sending him copies of minutes or memoranda.

2. Arranging for him to be called on as soon as anything occurs that may involve the reaction of any of the organization's publics or that may involve public notice.

3. Arranging for periodic (preferably monthly or oftener) meetings between officials of the client organization, the internal public relations executives, and the principal of the counseling firm. At these meetings the problems, considerations, events, and accomplishments encountered since the previous meeting should be discussed; all matters affecting the organization's human-climate functions should be evaluated and worked into ongoing plans; and decisions on future practices and activities should be made.

4. Setting methods for continuous review of the human-climate considerations and activities. If periodic reports are to be made to the client, what form should they be in, how often should they be made, what aspects of the effort should be emphasized?

5. Setting up channels for getting information before analyses, studies, or activities are begun. Someone within the organization should be designated as a liaison for information, or one person should be named as the source of information on each phase of the organization's operation.

6. Arranging for periodic briefing of the counsel on all pertinent phases of the organization's operations.

7. Establishing continuous communication between the organization and the counsel. Should the counsel send the client

copies of all correspondence he handles in connection with his service, or only on specific subjects or in specified connections? Should the counsel prepare a written report on each meeting with client personnel, for circulation to all concerned within the client organization and the counsel's firm?

Methods of payment

While in the considerations here we have been emphasizing services that involve the top management, it is also important for management to be familiar with billing arrangements for services that may be conducted on behalf of the internal department.

Often counsel and creative input for management will be combined with other services provided by the firm. Also, the ability to judge the value of a firm's service when it is embodied in the department's budget requests is important for management, just as it is in evaluating any other cost of operation.

Besides the wide variety of possible functions provided, there is a wide range in methods of charging for services.[1] There is also a wide variance in the rates charged, just as there is in other professions. Rates generally depend on the reputation and caliber of the counsel's organization, but do not necessarily reflect the quality of the service to be provided.

A prospective client should analyze the operating methods of the various firms being considered and the components included in various budget items at the same time that he evaluates the prices quoted. Otherwise, he may find that the service is a "blind" item.

In most cases where the counsel is on a continuous basis, the budget is set annually and the agreement runs for one-year periods. Sometimes the agreement is bound in a strictly legal contract; more often there is a covering letter citing the terms of the agreement, accepted by both parties; frequently there is merely a gentleman's agreement. Because of the confidential and intimate nature of this profession, disagreements over terms or payments are incompatible with good service, and it is widely considered that a gentleman's agreement is really the basis for every arrangement, whether there is a legal contract or not.

Selecting a counsel

The following are considerations in selecting a counsel beyond those that would normally be applied in selecting any service or personnel:

1. Would the firm have any conflicts of interest if it were to represent your organization?

For many years it was generally considered unwise to retain any firm in this field if it had a client in the same line of activity. This was based on the same concern over confidentiality of information in competitive areas that applies with advertising agencies. The concern was greatest when public relations firms were usually selected for product publicity programs, because of the great sensitivity of marketing executives over product and promotion secrecy.

There seems to be some lessening of this concern. It is now fairly common for one firm to represent both a trade association and an important member firm in that association. The ability to maintain confidentiality where competitive information could be involved is more widely accepted in such a relationship.

In addition, there seems to be some lessening of the taboo against representing competitive firms within the same industry. Much of this is due to the diversification of client firms into many fields, so that the number of their competitors is multiplied. Accordingly, it is not uncommon for one counseling firm to represent two organizations that compete, especially if the firm does not deal with divisions or subsidiaries that are competitive with each other.

It is still considered unwise to retain a counseling firm that represents another client with an opposing viewpoint on a basic issue, such as a manufacturer with a high level of smoke exhaust and an antipollution organization.

2. The most important criterion for judging a counseling firm is its reputation among the most discerning and objective observers: former clients, competitors and others in the field, responsible media, and banks. The sources to be checked most carefully for information on a firm should be those not provided by the firm itself.

Since there are two different bases for selection of a firm, the key points to be checked on its reputation will differ:

• For counseling and creative input, the caliber of mind and the character of the principal or principals who serve the organization are the overriding considerations.

• What is the status in the field as a whole of the principal who will serve your organization? Has he represented successfully and for a long period a number of substantial and discriminating clients?

• For the firm that is to be retained to carry out program functions, its ability in performing the various techniques to be employed is crucial.

3. It is wise to be suspicious of any presentation or solicitation that seems to be based on a formula or a composite of what has been done for other organizations. Dependence on formulas or emphasis on past work may indicate the firm lacks imagination and thinks in terms of setting up routine structures to follow. Since each client organization's needs and problems are different and the circumstances will vary considerably from any other, flexibility and openness of mind are important.

4. It is also wise to be suspicious of claims of results that the firm demonstrates.

First, emphasis on results indicates an emphasis on specific and tangible functions rather than on the breadth of thinking and creativity. Second, usually there are a number of elements that have gone into a successful effort, and it is important to question who really did what is claimed. How much of it was due to the sound judgment and effort of the client's own staff, for instance?

5. If the firm presents extensive reports on what it has done for other clients, it is wise to question whether that represents a revelation of confidences. If it is willing to talk freely about the problems of other clients and what has been done for them, it might be assumed that it will do the same about your organization if you become a client.

6. There are basically two types of firm in this field: those that are sales oriented, who concentrate most of their efforts on soliciting new clients; and those who are professionally service oriented, who concentrate their efforts on serving their clients and attracting new ones by reputation and performance.

Those firms that are constantly soliciting accounts tend to be sales oriented. It is wise to examine their record for retention of clients, turnover of personnel, reputation in the field, and other attributes.

The most effective counselors are professionals much like doctors and attorneys. They are able to confine their new-business efforts to building a reputation and to issuing modest informational materials to call attention to their availability and the services they provide.

chapter 62 Evaluating and guiding the human-climate program

BECAUSE of the growing tendency of professional managers to use quantifying techniques in evaluating all functions, there has been growing pressure to apply the same methods to human-climate functions. Since this field deals with the most intangible factors managers must cope with—human attitudes —it is understandable that it can evoke discomfort in a man who has been trained to be entirely practical and fact-oriented.[1]

However, there is danger that the more effort is made to apply standards of prediction and measurement, the more emphasis will be placed on the superficial, and the more difficult it will be to make progress against the real problems.

There are several reasons for this:

1. The greatest resource of the human-climate field is human intellect and creativeness. The very ability to perceive why people do not follow the expected and how they might be reached with messages that have not been projected previously is the greatest value a client can receive.

To the degree that direct measurements are attempted against

256

these attributes, there is danger that the unremarkable and the undistinguished—what has been done before and therefore can be measured—will be emphasized at the expense of the unique and the excellent.

If managements insist on being able to predict and measure quantitatively in human-climate areas, people who have responsibility in these areas will be inclined to confine themselves to things that are predictable and measurable, and the best thinking and creativity will be lost.

2. This field must deal with changes in attitude. It must lead its target, not follow it. The greatest source of problems and needs is *change.* If too much weight is given to what surveys and computer readouts show attitudes *were,* it is less likely that the program will have an effect on what they *will be.*

3. In obtaining data for quantified judgments, it is necessary to probe into the minds of people. The human mind is murky and its ramifications are multitudinous; and all the mental resources of the person are arrayed in defense of the individual's private thoughts and feelings.

It is not sound to assume that effective measurement of some attitudes indicates the possibility of accurately measuring all others. In any survey, interviewees' reactions are meaningful only when the subject is really meaningful to them: a major election, for instance. When queried about something less meaningful—such as acceptable profit margins of food processors—they may answer, but the validity and stability of their answers—especially numerically and over a period of time—are dubious.

Basing evaluation on judgment

In cases where a very tangible goal, such as obtaining publicity about products, is involved, the measurements can be reasonably specific. However, in the broad area of managing the human climate, it is extremely limiting and harmful to use a highly tangible measurement technique as a guide.

In every human-climate program some sort of evaluation is called for. Usually this is a judgment by the manager and the practitioner on what progress is being made toward the objectives that have been clearly established.

Aside from this, the differences are far greater than the similarities. No two programs should even be thought to be alike; it is individual differences and the relationships of human attitudes that make good public relations necessary and meaningful. To apply patterns from other programs is like using IBM cards to substitute for human relationships on a college campus or in a company's personnel program.

It is vital for the manager to keep in mind that often the most important result of sound judgment and practice in this field is what *does not happen*. Good judgment that prevents an organization from doing or saying something that would create an uproar, a backlash, or a government citation is obviously of great value. But, of course, it cannot be tabulated or quantified for evaluation.

Similarly—and increasingly, as the public becomes more educated, more sophisticated, and more skeptical—a low-key approach is likely to be most advisable. Such an approach by definition is less likely to create visible and tangible evidence. A quiet but effective program, for instance, of gaining the confidence of security analysts in a company's stock is more effective and more valuable than a flashy campaign with many meetings, much communications material, and full-page ads. Such a flashy program puts the analysts on their guard and may even increase their skepticism.

It should also be remembered that although practitioners in the human-climate field cannot any longer expect to be invisible—they must, indeed, be prepared for having a spotlight put on their functions by dissent groups, the SEC, or others—it is their function to develop visibility for others, and not for themselves. This means that proper functioning will work against a flashy result that the practitioner can show off, while it contributes importantly to the results that the management seeks.

Accordingly, the real and sound basis for evaluating in this field is the confidence the managers have in the people and their performance. As in the case of college professors or physicians, it is the feeling the client has for the judgment and the caliber of performance that counts and not a tabulation of functions performed. The client's sense of the advice he is getting and what is happening is the best basis of evaluation.

It is important to keep in mind that the interchange between an organization and its publics is a *relationship*. It has the characteristics of other types of relationship. A man does not value his relationship with his wife in terms of a tabulation of how many meals she prepares, how many pairs of socks she launders, or whether she has attended enough PTA meetings. He values the relationship in terms of the rapport they have together. And he counts on his judgment and his sense of human relationships to tell him whether it is a good relationship or a poor one.

Providing guidance

Directing the thrust of the program can involve a number of elements but generally these are the most effective:

1. Periodic meetings in which there is a frank and thorough two-way exchange of information and mutual briefing. At the same time this benefits both groups in performing their responsibilities, it is an important basis for the management's evaluation of the judgment, the integrity, and the ability of the staff people and counsel.

2. Reports on trends and developments, as a basis for discussion and review. Figures and tangible information should be used

to illuminate and support these reports and discussions, but not be the gist of them.

3. Getting readings from outsiders in a position to observe what is occurring in the field the organization is in, as well as within the organization itself. These outsiders often are in a good position to indicate the trend of the organization's human climate. They include others in the field you are in, editors of publications that deal with your field, financial experts whose responsibility it is to watch and evaluate organizations in your field, and perhaps government officials and faculty people who make a study of your field.

Proper evaluation goes back to the essentials:

• What makes up the organization's human climate?
• Why is that climate so important in determining its course?
• What are its problems?
• What are its opportunities?
• What are its resources and how can they be augmented to be sure the needs are well met?

It has been the purpose of this book to help the manager understand and assess these factors, and to know how to proceed in this essential area with confidence of success.

With the proper awareness of the essentiality of managing the human climate, a recognition of its particular difficulties, and the selection and guidance of the best people available, today's manager can face the great uncertainties and challenges of our turbulent society with reasonable assurance that he is indeed meeting his responsibilities as a manager.

Notes

CHAPTER 4

1. Speech at Pittsburgh, Pa., September 27, 1971; quoted in *Wall Street Journal,* December 8, 1971.

2. *U.S. News & World Report,* Oct. 8, 1973.

3. In 1970, 18.22 percent of all nonagricultural employment was in nonprofit fields, not including functions largely supportive of nonprofit institutions, such as "think tanks" and voluntary organizations, according to *The Statistical Abstract of the United States,* 1972, p. 219.

4. In addition to the widely publicized Harris and Opinion Research Corporation polls, one made for the Department of Commerce and published in the June 21, 1971, issue of *PR Reporter* is revealing:

Too few companies have too much power................... 61%
Large companies should be broken up...................... 45%
Business cold and impersonal 65%
Consumer not getting full dollar value................... 68%
Consumer not getting best possible products at least possible cost 85%
Industry primarily responsible for air and water pollution 80%
Close up pollution law violators 81%

5. *Public Relations News,* January 17, 1972.

6. "Who Should Police Environmental Advertising?" by Peter M. Sandman, *Columbia Journalism Review,* January–February 1972.

7. Ibid.

8. *Public Relations News,* December 6, 1971.

CHAPTER 8

1. Adapted from "Effective Management and the Human Factor," *Journal of Marketing,* January 1965.

CHAPTER 28

1. Philip Lesly. *Lesly's Public Relations Handbook* (Englewood Cliffs, N.J.: Prentice-Hall Inc., 1971). p. 518.
2. *The Gallagher Report*, New York, October 15, 1969.

CHAPTER 37

1. Bernard Berelson and Gary A. Steiner. *Human Behavior: An Inventory of Scientific Findings*. (New York: Harcourt, Brace and World, 1964).

CHAPTER 41

1. George Orwell. *Shooting an Elephant and Other Essays* (New York: Harcourt, Brace, & World, 1945).

CHAPTER 43

1. Pierre Martineau. *Motivation in Advertising* (New York: McGraw-Hill, 1957), pp. 128–29.
2. Rex F. Harlow. *Social Science in Public Relations* (New York: Harper, 1957), p. 46.

CHAPTER 45

1. *The Quill*, February 1970.

CHAPTER 49

1. Adapted from *Lesly's Public Relations Handbook*, ch. 35

CHAPTER 57

1. Ibid., ch. 2.

CHAPTER 61

1. Ibid., pp. 496–99.

CHAPTER 62

1. Ibid., p. 522.

Index

Index